The Mindful Manager

The Mindful Manager

SANDEEP ROY

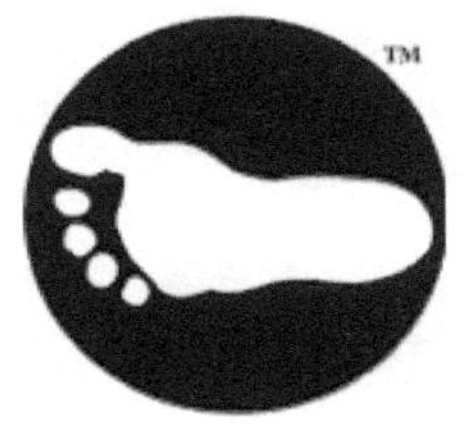

Bigfoot Publications
Because, there's a writer in everyone.

The Mindful Manager
Author : Sandeep Roy

First Published by
Bigfoot06 Publications (OPC) Pvt. Ltd.
1st floor, BSR Building near Vishal Mega Mart,
Daultabad Flyover, Laxman Vihar Phase 3,
Gurugram, Haryana (122001)
Website: www.bigfootpublications.in
Email: info@bigfootpublications.in

First Edition : February, 2024
© Sandeep Roy

ISBN Print Book - 9798884065307

Although the author and publisher have made every effort to ensure the accuracy and completeness of information contained in this book, we assume no responsibility for errors, inaccuracies, omissions, or any inconsistencies herein. Any slights on people, places, or organizations are unintentional.

Typeset in Garamond 12pt
by Yachika Prajapati For Bigfoot06 Publications

Printed in India

Table of Contents

PART - I

INTRODUCTION

In a lively metropolis teeming with busy people resided a youthful executive named Emma. Emma was known for her unwavering dedication to her work and her relentless pursuit of success. However, the mounting pressures and never-ending demands of her job had begun to take a toll on her well-being. She often found herself overwhelmed, mentally drained, and struggling to find a sense of balance in her life.

One day, while browsing through a local bookstore during her lunch break, Emma stumbled upon a book about mindfulness. Intrigued by the idea of finding inner peace amidst the chaos, she decided to give it a try. Little did she know that this decision would transform not only her own life but also the lives of those around her.

Now, let's explore some practical examples of how mindfulness can be incorporated into your daily life:

1. **Morning Mindful Breathing:** Start your day with a few minutes of intentional deep breathing. Find a quiet spot, close your eyes, and focus on the sensation of your breath entering and leaving your body. This simple practice can help you set a positive and calm tone for the day ahead.

2. **Mindful Meetings:** Instead of rushing through meetings with a scattered mind, practice mindful presence. Before each meeting, take a few moments to ground yourself by focusing on your breath or doing a quick body scan.

Engage fully in the discussions, listen attentively, and respond thoughtfully, fostering a more productive and meaningful exchange of ideas.

3. **Mindful Breaks:** Incorporate short mindfulness breaks throughout your workday. Whether it's a few minutes of stretching, a mindful walk outdoors, or even a brief meditation session, these breaks can rejuvenate your mind and help prevent burnout.

4. **Mindful Communication:** Practice mindful communication by truly listening to others without interrupting or preoccupying your mind with your response. Give your full attention to the person speaking, empathize with their perspective, and respond in a compassionate and understanding manner.

End-of-Day Reflection: Dedicate a few minutes at the end of each workday to reflect on your accomplishments and experiences. Allow yourself to acknowledge both the challenges you faced and the successes you achieved, all without judgment. This reflection time can help you gain insights, learn from your experiences, and let go of any lingering stress or tension.

CHAPTER 1
WHAT IS MINDFULNESS?

Mindfulness is a term that has been thrown around quite a bit in recent years, but what exactly does it mean? Essentially, mindfulness is the practice of being present and fully engaged in the current moment without judgment or distraction. It involves focusing your attention on your thoughts, feelings, and physical sensations and being aware of them without getting caught up in them or reacting to them.

For managers and workers alike, mindfulness can be a powerful tool for reducing stress, improving focus and productivity, and enhancing overall well-being. By practicing mindfulness, you can learn to manage your thoughts and emotions more effectively, stay calm and centered in the face of challenges, and make better decisions based on a clear and balanced perspective.

There are many different techniques and practices that can help cultivate mindfulness, including meditation, deep breathing, body scan exercises, and mindful movement (such as yoga or tai chi). Each of these approaches offers a unique way to bring attention to the present moment and develop a greater sense of awareness.

Meditation is one of the most well-known and widely practiced forms of mindfulness. By sitting quietly and focusing your attention on your breath or a specific point of focus, you can train your mind to become more present and less entangled in thoughts and distractions. Deep breathing exercises can also be effective in promoting relaxation and grounding the mind and body.

Body scan exercises involve systematically directing your attention to different parts of your body and noticing any sensations or tensions that may arise. This practice can help you develop a greater sense of bodily awareness and release any physical stress or discomfort.

Mindful movement practices like yoga or tai chi combine physical postures, breath control, and focused attention, creating a holistic experience that promotes both physical and mental well-being. These practices encourage you to be fully present in your body and cultivate a deep connection between your mind and physical sensations.

One of the most important aspects of mindfulness is developing a non-judgmental attitude towards yourself and others. This means recognizing and accepting your thoughts and emotions as they are without trying to change or suppress them. It also means being kind and compassionate towards yourself and others and practicing empathy and understanding in your interactions.

In the high-pressure environment of modern work culture, mindfulness can be a valuable tool for managers, workers, and owners alike. By cultivating a mindful approach to work and life, you can reduce stress, enhance focus and productivity, and improve your overall well-being. Mindfulness allows you to step back from the constant demands and distractions and find a sense of balance and clarity amidst the chaos.

So why not give it a try? Start small, with just a few minutes of mindful breathing or meditation each day, and see how it can benefit you and those around you. Incorporate mindfulness into your daily routine and observe the positive impact it has on your well-being and the quality of your work. Embrace the power of the present moment and unlock the potential for a more fulfilling and balanced life.

CHAPTER 2
WHY IS MINDFULNESS IMPORTANT FOR MANAGERS?

When you're a manager working in the hectic environment of day-to-day operations, it may be all too easy to get caught up in the frenzy and forget what's important. You are responsible for supervising your staff, keeping to the deadlines, and ensuring that your organization is successful in its endeavors. Nevertheless, in the middle of all of the hectic demands, it is very necessary to take a step back and engage in the practise of mindfulness in order to maintain a delicate balance between your personal life and your professional life.

The practise of being completely present and involved in the activity of the present moment is known as mindfulness. It gives you the ability to concentrate on the work at hand while keeping you aware of your thoughts and feelings without requiring you to cast judgment on them. As a manager, adding mindfulness to your daily activities may result in a wide variety of positive outcomes.

In the first place, practicing mindfulness improves your capacity to make decisions. You may have the capacity to observe things more clearly and make better judgments if you practice mindfulness and make it a part of your daily life. Mindfulness makes it possible for you to approach decision-making in a calm and objective manner, in contrast to the state of mind that results when emotions or stress obscure your thinking. Imagine, for example, that you are in the middle of a difficult circumstance in which a member of your team is having a hard time meeting an important deadline. Mindfulness encourages you to take a step back, evaluate the circumstance with objectivity, and think about several paths you may take to effectively help another person rather than responding on the spur of the moment.

The second benefit of cultivating mindfulness is an increase in one's capacity for effective communication. When dealing with other people, it encourages a stronger feeling of presence and alertness on your part. You are able to become a more engaged listener, capable of asking perceptive questions and reacting with thoughtfulness when you practice mindfulness. For instance, practicing mindfulness enables you to actually interact with the members of your team during team meetings rather than being consumed with your own thoughts or other external distractions. This creates an atmosphere that is favorable to open discourse and cooperation.

In addition, stress is an unavoidable aspect of the trip that a manager must take. Mindfulness, on the other hand, is a very useful skill for the successful management of stress. Through the practise of mindfulness, you may learn to separate yourself from the swirl of thoughts and feelings, which will enable you to notice them without being involved in them. This heightened awareness gives you the capacity to react to stress in a healthy way, so minimizing the negative impacts that stress has on your well-being and maximizing its positive ones. Imagine, for example, that you are in the midst of a race against the clock, and the amount of pressure continues to rise. You may restore your clarity and address the problem with a more relaxed perspective by introducing mindfulness activities such as deep breathing or meditation into your daily practice.

Additionally, mindfulness is associated with greater levels of productivity. When you are totally present and focused on the task at hand, your productivity and output will increase significantly. Being mindful enables you to avoid becoming sidetracked by irrelevant thoughts and activities, which in turn makes it easier for you to remain on track and accomplish what you set out to do. Take, for instance, the scenario in which you find yourself constantly giving in to the draw of checking emails or participating in activities related to social media while working on an important assignment. The practise of mindfulness raises your awareness of these distractions, which in turn enables you to intentionally refocus your attention on the work at hand. This, in turn, results in deliverables that are both more timely and of better quality.

Mindfulness plays an equally significant part in achieving a good balance between one's professional and personal life. It makes it possible for you to be completely present in both your personal and professional domains without leaving you feeling overwhelmed or exhausted. The practise of mindfulness may help you organize your priorities and make better use of your time and energy, giving you more breathing room to savor the experiences of your personal life while still meeting the demands of your professional obligations. For instance, instead of continuously checking work-related emails during your leisure time, practicing mindfulness urges you to detach and fully participate in things that offer you pleasure and relaxation, so cultivating a healthy balance in your life.

When you are in a managerial position, it is essential to set a good example for others. You may encourage the other members of your team to practice mindfulness by modeling the behavior for them in your own life. This, in turn, leads to a more pleasant and productive atmosphere at work, one in which everyone has the chance to flourish and grow. For example, beginning team meetings with a quick mindfulness practice may assist everyone in shifting into a frame of mind that is more focused and in the here and now. You may urge your team to incorporate mindfulness into their own work routines by practicing the tenets of mindfulness yourself and demonstrating the advantages of doing so.

In today's high-pressure, fast-paced work climate, mindfulness may be an extremely helpful tool for managers. Through cultivating mindfulness, one may improve their ability to make choices, improve their ability to interact with others, better manage stress, raise their level of productivity, and have a good work-life balance. When you make mindfulness a regular part of your life, not only do you become a more productive and satisfied manager, but you also create an atmosphere that encourages the expansion and achievement of both yourself and the members of your team.

CHAPTER 3
THE BENEFITS OF PRACTICING MINDFULNESS IN THE WORKPLACE

The advantages of cultivating a thoughtful attitude in one's professional life are genuinely astonishing. Mindfulness acts as a strong tool for managers, employees, owners, and manufacturers alike in today's fast-paced and high-pressure workplaces, allowing them to establish a harmonic balance between their professional and personal lives. Mindfulness entails paying attention to one's thoughts, feelings, and surroundings, as well as developing the ability to respond rather than react to a variety of events. It is characterized by an absence of judgment and distraction in the present moment when the practitioner is completely present.Increased productivity is one of the most important benefits that practitioners of mindfulness in the workplace report experiencing. When we train ourselves to be aware, we train ourselves to become completely involved in the activities that we are now doing, which enables us to concentrate more intently on the things that need to be done. Because of this heightened level of presence and attention, we are able to do things more quickly, with fewer mistakes, and with a better overall feeling of pleasure. Imagine, for example, a manager who is working on a difficult project but still manages to find time to practice mindfulness. They are able to break down the project into small pieces, efficiently prioritize their work, and handle each component with clarity and concentration if they remain completely present and attentive, which eventually leads to a more successful end.Another beneficial result of practicing mindfulness on the job is an increase in one's ability to communicate more effectively. When we are attentive, we improve our ability to listen to others, really comprehend their viewpoints, and react in a way that is both intelligent and helpful. This improved communication skill set has the potential to drastically cut down on disagreements, make cooperation more effective, and provide a more upbeat working atmosphere. Think about, for instance, a meeting of the team in which everyone is engaging in mindful practices. Because every member of the team is fully present and engaged in attentive listening to the thoughts and perspectives expressed by their fellow team members, the ensuing conversation is more inclusive and conducive to collaborative problem-solving.The mindfulness practice that we engage in may also have a significant effect on the mental and physical well-being that we experience on the job. It is common for professional situations to be associated with high levels of stress, which may lead to the production of cortisol, a hormone that is associated with adverse consequences for our health. The practice of mindfulness may be a powerful tool for relieving stress, enabling us to better control the impact that stress has on our lives. We may reduce the negative impacts of stress on our bodies and enjoy increased immune function, higher-quality sleep, and an overall enhanced sense of well-being if we practice mindfulness and remain present in the here and now while also being conscious of our thoughts and feelings. For example, a worker who adds mindfulness practices to their daily routine may find that they are better prepared to face hard deadlines or demanding circumstances as they are able to notice and address stress triggers before they escalate. This is because they are better able to recognize and treat stress triggers before they become more severe.In addition, cultivating mindfulness in the workplace encourages the development of empathetic and compassionate attitudes. When we are attentive, we increase our chances of connecting with other people on a deeper level and of displaying compassion, patience, and understanding in our interactions with them. This helps to create a healthy culture at work, one in which people feel appreciated, supported, and valued in their roles. An example of how a manager who practices mindfulness can demonstrate empathy is by actively listening to an employee who is struggling with a personal issue, offering support and understanding, and working together to find a solution that accommodates both the employee's needs and the demands of the work environment. This is just one example of how a manager who practices mindfulness can demonstrate empathy.Mindfulness is a technique that helps people create a heightened sense of self-awareness as well as a nonjudgmental focus on the present moment. Mindfulness, when practiced in the workplace, has several advantages that, when combined, contribute to both the individual and collective well-being of employees as well as the overall success of the business.The capacity to improve one's attention and concentration is one of the primary advantages of practicing mindfulness on the job. Distractions are everywhere in today's environment, from conflicting objectives and deadlines to constant emails and messages that pop up on your phone. People may train their thoughts to remain focused on the topic at hand by introducing mindfulness practices into their regular work routines. This helps people reduce distractions and improve their general attention. This, in turn, leads to an increase in productivity as well as the capability to accomplish activities with more efficiency and precision.In addition to this, cultivating mindfulness helps one become more resilient in the face of adversity and failure. When working in an atmosphere with a lot of pressure, you will inevitably experience tension, frustration, and unforeseen roadblocks. Those who engage in the practice of mindfulness, on the other hand, are better prepared to deal with adverse circumstances. They are able to confront issues with a cool and controlled mentality if they cultivate an attitude of non-judgmentalism and a concentration on the present moment. This enables them to respond rather than react impulsively to the obstacles they face. This capability to traverse obstacles with resilience not only decreases stress levels but also fosters a proactive and solutions-oriented attitude toward problem-solving.One further benefit of practicing mindfulness at work is the positive influence it has on creative problem-solving and innovative thinking. When people are completely present in the moment and in sync with their own thoughts and feelings, they are better able to access the creative potential that is inside them. The practice of mindfulness makes room for novel points of view, novel ideas, and original methods of approaching challenging situations. Individuals may overcome mental obstacles, release their creative potential, and contribute to a culture of innovation inside a business if they adopt a mindfulness practice and make it a part of their lives.In addition, developing good leadership skills requires a significant contribution from mindfulness. Leaders who are mindful have a heightened sense of self-awareness as well as a higher level of emotional intelligence and empathy. They have a better awareness of both their own capabilities and their limits, as well as the requirements and concerns of the other members of their team. Because of this, they are able to lead with sincerity as well as compassion, and empathy. A mindful leader is one who cultivates a work atmosphere that is supportive and inclusive, in which team members feel valued and heard and are driven to achieve to the best of their abilities.In addition, practicing mindfulness at work may have a beneficial effect on professional relationships and teamwork. When people engage in mindfulness practice, it causes them to become more attentive and present in their relationships with their coworkers. This heightened sense of presence makes it easier to communicate effectively, to listen actively, and to get a better understanding of the viewpoints held by others. Improved teamwork, synergy, and collaborative problem-solving may result when a business promotes a culture of mindfulness among its employees. This can lead to the cultivation of strong, trustworthy connections among the members of a team.Practicing mindfulness in the workplace is beneficial to one's health as a whole and to maintaining a healthy work-life balance. Individuals who regularly practice mindfulness are more likely to establish clearer boundaries between their personal and professional lives, which in turn makes it possible to lead lives that are more purposeful and well-balanced. Individuals may remove themselves from the pressures associated with their jobs during their leisure time by engaging in mindful practice. This results in enhanced contentment and fulfillment in both the professional and personal spheres of life. This balance not only promotes well-being but also reduces the risk of burnout and increases overall productivity over the long run.The practice of mindfulness in the workplace is associated with a multitude of positive outcomes. It improves one's ability to concentrate, as well as resilience, creativity, leadership, and general well-being. Businesses are able to foster a work environment that is not only healthier but also more productive and gratifying for all employees if they cultivate a culture of mindfulness inside their firm and make the practice of mindfulness part of their regular work routines.

PART - II
THE MINDFUL MANAGER'S MINDSET

In the heart of a bustling metropolis, there was a dynamic manager named Alex. Alex had always been ambitious and driven, constantly striving to achieve success in the fast-paced business world. However, as responsibilities piled up and challenges intensified, Alex began to realize the importance of self-awareness in maintaining a balanced and effective leadership style.

One evening, while reflecting on the day's events, Alex came across an article that emphasized the transformative power of self-awareness in managerial roles. Intrigued, Alex delved deeper into the subject, determined to enhance personal growth and optimize team dynamics through self-awareness.

Practical examples of how self-awareness can be applied in a managerial context include:

1. **Feedback and Reflection:** Encourage a culture of open feedback and self-reflection within the team. By actively seeking feedback from team members and reflecting on one's own actions, managers can gain valuable insights into their leadership style and make necessary adjustments to improve effectiveness.

2. **Emotional Regulation:** Develop strategies for emotional regulation during high-pressure situations. Self-aware managers can identify when emotions might interfere with decision-making and take proactive steps to regain

composure. This may include taking short breaks, practicing mindfulness techniques, or seeking support from trusted colleagues.

3. **Adaptive Communication:** Understand and adapt communication styles to meet the needs of individual team members. Self-aware managers recognize their own communication preferences and biases, allowing them to tailor their approach to facilitate effective communication and build stronger relationships within the team.

4. **Continual Learning and Growth:** Embrace a growth mindset and a commitment to ongoing learning. Self-aware managers understand their strengths and limitations and actively seek opportunities for personal and professional development. They engage in continuous learning, whether through workshops, coaching, or seeking out new perspectives, to enhance their leadership capabilities.

CHAPTER 4
THE IMPORTANCE OF SELF-AWARENESS

Self-awareness has emerged as one of the most crucial attributes for successful managers to possess in today's fast-paced and continuously changing business environment. Self-awareness is one of the most important characteristics for successful managers to possess. It requires having a comprehensive understanding of one's own thoughts, emotions, and behaviors, in addition to the influence that these things have on the lives of other people. Self-awareness helps managers recognize areas in which they have room for personal improvement, successfully regulate their emotions, and interact more effectively with the teams they supervise, all of which are benefits to the organization as a whole. Let's go a little more into the significance of maintaining a balanced level of self-awareness, shall we?One of the most important advantages of cultivating self-awareness is the ability to perceive one's own prejudices and biases, which is why developing this talent is so important. No one is immune to harboring some degree of bias, regardless of whether or not they are aware of their own preconceptions. Self-aware managers, on the other hand, are able to recognize their own biases and work actively to overcome them. Self-aware managers are more likely to be successful. When dealing with individuals who come from a number of various cultures and backgrounds, it may be difficult for managers to effectively lead and communicate with their staff because of the diversity of those cultures and backgrounds. In diverse workplaces, this becomes an extremely important aspect to take into account. If managers are ready to confront and overcome their own unconscious prejudices, they have the opportunity to create an environment that is welcoming, courteous, and celebratory of diversity, all while fostering an atmosphere that stimulates collaboration.In addition to this, managers who have a great sense of self-awareness are better able to regulate their own moods and behaviors. When working under intense conditions, it's easy for emotions to swiftly spiral out of control, which may leave managers feeling overloaded and anxious about their jobs. Self-aware managers, on the other hand, are able to recognize when their feelings are starting to get in the way of their judgment and take the steps necessary to rectify the situation. As a direct consequence of their enhanced degree of self-awareness, they are able to take preventative actions in order to maintain appropriate control over their emotions. It may include doing something as simple as taking a little break to regain composure, engaging in mindfulness activities to cultivate a more tranquil state of mind, or seeking assistance from reliable coworkers or mentors. Taking a short pause is an effective strategy for regaining composure and sanity. If they are able to keep their emotions under control, managers are in a better position to lead their people with clarity and fortitude, as well as make rational judgments about the situation at hand.In addition, having a strong sense of self-awareness is one of the most important factors in enhancing communication among teams and groups. When managers have a thorough understanding of their own communication style as well as how it may be interpreted by others, they are better able to alter their approach to better meet the requirements of the members of their team. This is because they are better able to understand the needs of their team members. Effective communication requires not just the ability to convey information in a fashion that is easily comprehended by others but also in a manner that evokes an emotional response from those individuals. Managers that are self-aware have the opportunity to use this understanding to their advantage by using appropriate language, offering the necessary context, and actively listening to their team members. If managers tailor their communication style to the tastes and requirements of their team, they may be able to build stronger relationships, resolve arguments more rapidly, and ensure that everyone is aligned and working towards common goals.It is likely one of the most crucial abilities for managers to acquire throughout the course of their careers, and that skill is self-awareness. When managers have a solid understanding of the thoughts, emotions, and behaviors of their staff members, they are better equipped to identify opportunities for their own personal and professional growth. They are aware of both their capabilities and their limits, which encourages an attitude of lifelong education and contributes to their upward movement. They are able to accomplish this because they have self-awareness. In addition to this, it equips managers with the skills essential to regulating their own emotions, which ensures that they are able to keep calm and remain sensible even when they are under a great deal of strain. This power to manage oneself serves as a source of inspiration and stability for the members of their team, which helps them grow in spite of the challenges that are provided to them.Self-awareness is a vital trait for managers who want to perform at the highest potential in their professions, and it is one of the most difficult qualities to cultivate. Managers who work to improve their self-awareness may find that doing so gives them the capacity to negotiate their own biases, maintain effective control of their emotions, and communicate with more clarity and empathy. Managers who have a high degree of self-awareness are able to keep their cool, continue to concentrate on the work at hand, and effectively carry out their obligations even when the stakes are very high. Managers have the power to construct a wholesome and encouraging work culture that fosters growth, collaboration, and success by adopting self-awareness as a fundamental characteristic of their leadership style and making it a major component of their management strategy. This allows managers to produce a healthy and supportive work environment that supports development, cooperation, and success.

CHAPTER 5
THE POWER OF POSITIVE THINKING

In today's fast-paced workplaces, it is easy to lose sight of how important it is to have a positive state of mind in order to be productive. Even if we have the propensity to associate it with personal development and contentment outside of the job, its worth in the professional realm is just as substantial as the value it has outside of that context. Your state of mind and the manner in which you respond to certain occurrences as a manager have the potential to have a substantial impact on the performance of both your team and the company as a whole.

When you have a positive attitude, you are more likely to confront challenges with optimism and have the capacity to recover quickly from failures. This point of view makes it possible for you to effectively handle difficult situations, which in turn makes it possible for you to find creative solutions to problems that, under other circumstances, would have been insurmountable. Your positive attitude not only inspires confidence in your team members but also makes them more self-motivated and hopeful about the future. This, in turn, pushes them to confront challenges with a fervor and zeal that they may not have previously had.

On the other side, having a negative view might be detrimental to not just your own productivity but also the morale of your team. When you focus on the negative aspects of a situation, it is all too easy to become caught up in feelings of aggravation, stress, and despair. Because of this, it is all the more crucial to avoid focusing on the negative aspects of a scenario. This not only has an influence on your own personal performance, but it also permeates the workplace, which eventually results in decreased productivity, increased turnover, and an overall sense of discontent among your workers.

In light of this, as a manager, how can you make it a priority to cultivate a more positive state of mind? The process begins with you developing a heightened awareness of your thoughts and attitudes, which is the first stage. If you become aware that you are experiencing negative ideas, you should make an urgent effort to reframe them in a manner that is more positive. This should be done as soon as you become aware that you are having negative thoughts. Think about changing the way you look at challenges so that you don't see them as a sign that you've lost but rather as an opportunity for you to grow as a person and go forward in your career. When you shift the way you look at things, you not only open yourself up to a whole new world of possibilities, but you also give yourself the ability to confront challenges with a heightened sense of determination.

Gratitude meditation is yet another crucial element that should be included in positive thinking. Take some time out of your day to reflect on the things that you have to be grateful for, whether it be the support of your team, a challenging project that challenges your skills, or even simply the sunshine that is streaming through the window of your office. Give thanks for all of the things that you have in your life. You will be able to redirect your focus away from negative thoughts and toward the more positive aspects of your profession and life if you participate in this exercise. It encourages feelings of thankfulness as well as happiness, both of which are important contributors to the growth of an overall more optimistic view.

It is essential to be conscious of the idea that anything wonderful has the potential to spread rapidly. As the manager, it is incumbent upon you to set an example for the rest of the team, both in terms of your manner and your degree of excitement. If you approach your work with a positive attitude from the beginning, it will be much simpler for the rest of your team to do the same. When you go to work in an environment that is encouraging and motivating, you are more likely to be productive, engaged, and motivated, all of which are helpful not just to the business but also to your own personal well-being. If you exude positivity and serve as a model for others on the team to emulate, you will cause a chain reaction that will have an impact on the performance of the whole group.

It is impossible to exaggerate how important it is to have the capacity to think positively in one's professional life. A manager's ability to become more productive in their role and to have a greater sense of personal satisfaction may be improved through the development of a positive attitude. If you adopt an optimistic attitude toward challenging tasks, reframe hurdles as opportunities, nurture an attitude of gratitude, and lead by example, you may be able to create a positive climate at work that is favorable to success for both you and your team. This atmosphere may be conducive to success because it will be conducive to success for both of you. Embracing the power of positive thinking not only contributes to your own achievement but also multiplies the triumphs that your team as a whole achieves, which eventually leads to a more encouraging and prosperous future.

CHAPTER 6
DEVELOPING A GROWTH MINDSET

As a manager, it is essential to have a growth mindset. A growth mindset is a belief that you can develop your abilities, skills, and intelligence through hard work, effort, and perseverance. It is the opposite of a fixed mindset, which is the belief that your abilities and intelligence are fixed and cannot be changed.

Having a growth mindset is important because it allows you to embrace challenges, learn from failures, and push yourself to grow and improve. It also helps you to develop resilience, perseverance, and a positive attitude towards change.

Here are some tips for developing a growth mindset:

1. **Embrace challenges:** Instead of avoiding challenges, embrace them. Challenges are an opportunity to learn and grow. When you face a challenge, ask yourself what you can learn from it and how you can use it to improve. When it comes to both, one's personal and professional growth, having a mentality that is open to new challenges is one of the most distinguishing characteristics of successful people. They don't run away from challenges but instead embrace them as chances for personal development, expansion of knowledge, and enhancement of skills. Adopting this strategy as a manager may give you the ability to guide your team through difficult circumstances, inspire resilience, and promote a culture of continual progress.

It is normal to feel some level of unease or even panic when confronted with a difficult situation. On the other hand, a growth-oriented manager is one who, rather than giving in to negative feelings, acknowledges the potential advantages that might be brought about by adversity. You may show that you are eager to push yourself beyond your comfort zone and increase your talents by actively seeking out and accepting challenges. Your team will get a strong message if they see that you do not fear difficulties but rather welcome them with open arms and strive to overcome them.

You may change your emphasis from the possible negative features of a task to the good results that might be accomplished by recasting the issue as an opportunity for learning and progress. Because of this transformation in mentality, you are now able to approach difficulties with a feeling of curiosity and open-mindedness, searching for answers and tactics that may move you and your team ahead.

Let's explore an example. Imagine that you are in charge of a group that has been assigned the creation of a new product. Unanticipated challenges, such as resource limitations, technological concerns, or changes in the target market, appear as you make progress on the project. Rather than allowing themselves to get disheartened, a manager who thrives on adversity would see these obstacles as instructive learning opportunities.

In this situation, you could urge your team to see the obstacles as chances to innovate and improve their problem-solving abilities by encouraging them to see the challenges as opportunities. You'll be able to tap into the collective brain of your team in order to come up with original ideas for problem-solving if you create a culture that encourages collaboration and fosters an atmosphere in which people aren't afraid to speak their minds or take sensible risks.

Accepting difficulties requires a mentality that is committed to making steady progress toward one's goals. It is crucial for you as a manager to take some time to think about the difficulties you confront and to learn from those difficulties. Spend some time analyzing which aspects performed effectively and which ones may need some tweaking. You may improve your ability to solve problems and make better decisions in the future by reflecting on your past experiences and drawing meaningful conclusions from those reflections.

For instance, let's imagine you're tasked with managing a varied team of people who have varying points of view, and you run into some difficulties. As you reflect on this experience, you may come to the conclusion that there is a need for enhanced communication as well as a deeper awareness of the distinctive abilities and methods of functioning that each member of your team has. With this information in hand, you will be able to modify your approach to leadership and put tactics into action that will result in improved teamwork and cohesiveness.

The attitude of welcoming and thriving in the face of adversity may be developed not just by a person but also by a group of people working together. You have the ability to inspire the members of your team to see problems as opportunities for personal growth and professional advancement if you are a manager. Create an atmosphere in which errors are seen as chances for learning rather than failures, and be sure to provide your team with both support and direction as they work to overcome the challenges they face.

You can motivate your team to rise to the occasion by taking on issues head-on and setting a positive example for them to follow. This kind of thinking contributes to the development of a culture that is both resilient and adaptable, one in which people have the sense that they are free to experiment, think creatively, and push the limits of what is possible.

The mentality of welcoming and excelling in the face of adversity is one of the most important success factors for managers and the teams they oversee. Managers may encourage resiliency, inventiveness, and continual improvement in their employees by encouraging them to perceive setbacks as opportunities for development and learning. Challenges may be transformed into stepping stones to greater accomplishments if they are met with an attitude of contemplation, teamwork, and positivity. Therefore, the next time you are faced with a difficulty, be sure to remember to accept it, look for the lessons it contains, and utilize it as a driving force for both your personal and professional development.

2. **Learn from failures:** Failure is not a setback but an opportunity to learn and grow. When you fail, take the time to reflect on what went wrong and what you can do differently next time. Use failure as a stepping stone to success.

The word "failure" is often connected with pejorative connotations, feelings of letdown, and obstacles. However, successful people and effective managers are aware that falling short of one's goals is not the end of the road but rather a priceless chance for personal development and professional advancement. Failure may be turned into a stepping stone to success if it is accepted and used as a stimulus for personal growth and development.

When confronted with adversity, it is essential to establish a mentality that prioritizes learning and introspection. Take a step back and conduct an impartial analysis of the issue rather than wallowing in the negative feelings that always accompany a failed attempt. Keep an eye out for insightful takeaways and significant lessons that may be gained from the event.

When you take the time to reflect on past setbacks, you give yourself the opportunity to better comprehend what transpired and the factors that led to them. It's possible that improper planning, inefficient communication, or a lack of resources contributed to the failure of a project. By isolating these contributing elements, you will be able to devise solutions to address them and protect yourself from making the same errors in the future.

Take, for instance, the scenario in which you are in charge of supervising a group that is tasked with introducing a brand-new marketing initiative. The campaign does not achieve its goals, which leads to a low level of consumer involvement and a small amount of customer reaction. Take this chance to reflect on what went wrong rather than wallowing in your dissatisfaction with the outcome. Determine what led to the poor success of the campaign, such as a lack of market research, an imprecise message, or insufficient marketing, and then work to address those aspects. You may establish a plan of action to enhance your strategy for future campaigns if you first acknowledge these limitations and then admit that you have them.

Getting criticism from others and considering other points of view is an essential part of learning from mistakes. Participate in conversations with other members of your team, your coworkers, or your mentors in order to get new ideas and other points of view. Their insights, observations, and comments might provide helpful views that may have been missed in the process.

In addition, it is essential to cultivate a culture in which failure is not seen as something to be ashamed of but rather as an inherent component of the educational process. You should make it a point to encourage the members of your team to be upfront about their mistakes and the lessons they've taken away from them. Because of this, an atmosphere of psychological safety is created, one in which people have the confidence to experiment with new ideas, take innovative risks, and gain knowledge from their blunders.

Take, for illustration purposes, the scenario of a product development team working on a new software release. In spite of their best efforts, the release is plagued with severe flaws and gets unfavorable comments from users. Instead of lingering on the loss, the team decides to perform a post-mortem investigation, in which each member of the team takes part, to investigate the factors that led to the loss. They have an open discussion about the things that they have discovered, and they devise strategies to improve their quality assurance procedures and user testing for their next projects.

The experience of failure may be a potent source of motivation as well as a driver of personal development. It highlights our limits as well as the areas in which we may progress. When you adopt a growth mindset and open yourself up to the possibility of failing, it enables you to cultivate resilience and persistence, which in turn enables you to recover from setbacks in a more powerful and determined manner than before.

It is essential for a manager to set a good example and communicate the challenges and setbacks they have faced in their careers. You may exhibit vulnerability and honesty by talking openly about your past mistakes and the things you've picked up from those experiences. Your team will become more trustworthy as a result of this, and they will be more likely to accept that failure is an inherent part of the path to success.

Failure should not be seen as a setback but rather as a stepping stone to the eventual achievement. It is possible for managers to instill in their teams a culture of continual improvement, creativity, and resilience through the application of lessons learned from previous mistakes. Recognize the value of setbacks as learning experiences, actively seek others' perspectives, and devise methods to navigate difficult situations. Keep in mind that the most successful people and organizations are those who have experienced failure but have been able to turn that experience into a driver of development and accomplishment. Therefore, the next time you are confronted with failure, think of it as a necessary and instructive step on the road to success.

3. **Practice perseverance:** Perseverance is the key to success. It is the ability to keep going even when things get tough. When you face obstacles, don't give up. Keep pushing forward, and you will eventually overcome them.

Perseverance is the steadfast resolve to continue pursuing your objectives and dreams, especially in the face of hardship. It is sometimes referred to as the secret ingredient that separates those who succeed from those who fail. It is a trait that differentiates individuals who are successful in realizing their goals from others who are unable to do so. As a manager, it is crucial for you to practice endurance not only for your own personal development but also for the purpose of inspiring and encouraging your team to overcome problems and achieve new heights.

Both in your personal life and in your professional life, you will inevitably face challenges and failures. They may manifest themselves in a variety of ways, including the failure of a project, being constrained financially, or even being a personal issue. Perseverance, on the other hand, really shows its worth at times like this since that's when it's put to the test.

When confronted with challenges, it is essential to have a positive outlook and resist the urge to get disheartened. Rather than seeing obstacles as impediments to your progress, embrace them as chances for personal development and improvement. You have the ability to turn obstacles into stepping stones on the path to success just by shifting your attitude.

Consider the life of Thomas Edison, who was responsible for the development of the first electric light bulb. It is believed that in order for him to finally achieve success, he had to endure a great deal of hardship and struggle. When questioned about his previous unsuccessful endeavors, the legendary inventor Thomas Edison famously remarked, "I have not failed. I've just discovered 10,000 different ways in which it won't function. Because of his constant determination, he was able to overcome obstacles and finally bring about a change in the world with the innovation that he created.

For someone to persevere, they need to be resilient, determined, and have a strong conviction in their own skills. It is the capacity to go on regardless of the circumstances, even when the deck is stacked against you. Your dogged determination is a beacon of hope for those under your management on the team. They will be inspired to adopt a similar mentality and strive for perfection when they see how tenacious you are in the face of obstacles.

Furthermore, developing persistence allows you to build key abilities such as problem-solving, flexibility, and ingenuity. These qualities may be developed through practice. When you are faced with challenges, you are compelled to think creatively and investigate several other options for resolving the problem. Your problem-solving skills will improve as a result of this, and your team will also develop a culture of innovation and continual growth as a result of the encouragement this provides.

Imagine for a moment that you are the leader of a project that has suddenly seen significant changes in its funding. You have shown tenacity by not giving up or lowering the quality of the work; rather, you have investigated alternate financing sources, reevaluated the scope of the project, and engaged with stakeholders to discover innovative solutions. Despite the first setback, the fact that you are dedicated and refuse to be discouraged inspires your team to join together, think of solutions that do not immediately spring to mind, and achieve success.

The trait of perseverance cannot be developed in isolation; rather, it calls for support and the participation of others. It is crucial for a manager to cultivate a supportive atmosphere within their team in which members feel empowered to work together to address obstacles. It is important to promote open communication, provide direction and resources, recognize and celebrate even the smallest of accomplishments along the path, and so on. You may strengthen your team's capacity for collective endurance by cultivating a sense of togetherness and shared purpose among its members.

In addition, persistence does not mean going through the motions without pausing for thought or making necessary adjustments. It is essential to take stock of your advancements, reflect on and gains wisdom from your experiences, and adjust your tactics appropriately. Sometimes it's vital to be flexible and ready to pivot or shift direction when it becomes required in order to maintain endurance. It is about maintaining a firm dedication to the destination while keeping an open mind on the specifics of how to get there.

It is very necessary for one's personal and professional success to develop the habit of persistence. It is the unflinching determination to go on despite the challenges and failures that may be encountered along the way. Your tenacity not only gives you the ability to triumph over obstacles, but it also acts as an example for the others on your team to follow in your footsteps. You can build an atmosphere in which people can thrive, inventions can develop, and objectives can be realized if you cultivate a culture of tenacity and resilience. Therefore, you should acknowledge the power of persistence, keep your attention fixed on the goals you've set for yourself, and never undervalue the significance of your unyielding determination.

4. **Develop a positive attitude towards change:** Change is inevitable, and it can be scary. But it is also an opportunity for growth and improvement. Instead of resisting change, embrace it. Look for the opportunities it presents and focus on the positive aspects of the change.

In today's rapidly advancing world, one of the most important skills one can acquire is the ability to have a positive attitude toward change. Both in one's personal life and in one's professional life, one must always be prepared for change. It is essential for you as a manager to be able to welcome change and guide your staff through it if you want to achieve success and maintain a competitive advantage in an environment that is always shifting and evolving.

Change may manifest itself in a variety of ways, including reorganizational restructuring, developments in technology, the introduction of new rules or processes, or alterations in the general tendencies of the market. Employees often experience anxiety, reluctance, and uncertainty in response to change. You may, however, cultivate an atmosphere that is conducive to expansion, creativity, and flexibility in your organization by creating a favorable attitude toward change.

In order to cultivate a positive attitude toward change, one of the most important things to do is accept it rather than fight against it. Consider the possibilities for personal development and advancement that come with change rather than perceiving it as a nuisance or a potential danger. The ability to adapt and grow as a result of experience and exposure to new situations and circumstances is one of the many benefits of change.

Consider the scenario of a manager guiding a group of employees through the process of switching to a new software system. The manager welcomes the change rather than seeing it as a burden or more work and instead sees it as a chance to simplify procedures, improve efficiency, and give members of the team new tools and skills. The manager may build a feeling of enthusiasm and motivation among the team by concentrating on the good parts of the shift and explaining the advantages that will result from the change. This will make the transition go more smoothly and result in greater success.

Keeping an open mind is another essential component of cultivating a disposition favorable toward change. Maintain an open mind to the novel concepts, points of view, and opportunities that change presents. Recognize that looking at things from a variety of perspectives may result in creativity and advancement. You should actively listen to the feedback provided by your team members and encourage them to share their opinions and concerns with you. You may develop a sense of ownership and cooperation among employees by including them in the process of change and rewarding the contributions they make. This will create a good atmosphere that is conducive to accepting change.

Effective communication is another skill that is very necessary during times of transition. It is helpful to ease fear and uncertainty among team members through clear and honest communication. It would be helpful if you could provide frequent updates, explain the rationale for the change, and respond to any concerns or questions that may arise. You can foster trust and make sure that everyone is on the same page by keeping everyone informed and including them in the process. This will boost the probability that the transition will be successful.

Additionally, in order to cultivate a good attitude about change, one must concentrate on the possibilities that are presented by the change. The process of change often paves the way for new opportunities, development, and improvements. Encourage your team to look beyond the problems that will be caused by the change and discover the benefits that will come from it. This may include gaining new knowledge and abilities, taking on more duties, or investigating new markets and prospects.

For instance, if your company decides to restructure itself, this may result in changes to the dynamics of teams or the reporting structures already in place. Place more emphasis on the chances for professional progression, cross-functional partnerships, or enhanced autonomy rather than obsessing over the possible disruptions that may occur. You may encourage your team to accept change with excitement and resilience by turning the emphasis of the conversation to the good outcomes that will result from the change.

Lastly, setting a good example for others is essential to cultivating a positive attitude toward change. Your demeanor and outlook as a manager have a significant impact on the mentality of the team members you are responsible for. Exhibit a positive outlook, the capacity to adjust, and a readiness to accept change in oneself. Tell us about some of your own experiences with effective change management, and be sure to emphasize the positive outcomes that came about as a consequence of being open to new experiences. When members of your team perceive that you have a positive attitude, they are more likely to adopt the same attitude toward the changes that are being implemented.

In order to be a good leader and ensure the success of a business, it is vital to have a positive attitude toward change. It is essential to cultivate a positive attitude toward change by concentrating on possibilities, retaining open-mindedness, embracing change rather than fighting against it, having an open mind, and maintaining efficient communication. You may establish an atmosphere that is conducive to innovation, development, and adaptation in your community by encouraging a culture that is open to change. Therefore, accept change as a chance for advancement and motivate your team to approach it with optimism and resiliency in order to succeed.

5. **Practice self-reflection:** Self-reflection is essential for personal growth and development. Take the time to reflect on your strengths and weaknesses, and identify areas where you can improve. Use this information to set goals and develop a plan for growth.

Personal growth and development are best served by one of the most effective tools available: reflective thinking. It entails pausing for a moment, turning your attention within, and critically analyzing your behaviors, emotions, and ideas. If you are a manager, engaging in regular self-reflection may have tremendous advantages not just for your personal development but also for the progress of your team and the overall accomplishments of the business.

Reflecting on oneself enables one to get a more comprehensive view of oneself, including one's own capabilities and limitations. It is possible to optimize your effectiveness as a manager by capitalizing on your strengths after doing an honest evaluation of your talents. In addition, being aware of your shortcomings helps you pinpoint the areas in which you need improvement and devise strategies that can expedite your development.

For instance, by engaging in some self-reflection, you may come to the realization that your greatest strengths lie in the areas of strategic thinking and problem-solving. Recognizing this, you have the ability to assign more operational chores to other members of your team who thrive in those areas. This will enable you to concentrate on your strengths and have a bigger influence overall. On the other side, if you discover that one of your weaknesses is the ability to delegate tasks effectively, you may make it a goal of yours to enhance your abilities in delegation and look for chances to practice and become better at it.

Your values, beliefs, and the things that drive you may all be better understood by doing some self-reflection. When you have a good grasp of what motivates you, you will be able to make choices and take actions that are congruent with your fundamental values, which will lead to more authenticity and a sense of accomplishment in your managerial job. When your behaviors are consistent with the things that are important to you, you foster an atmosphere of trust and positivity in the workplace.

In addition, engaging in self-reflection helps one become more self-aware, which is an essential quality for successful leadership. When you are conscious of your own ideas, feelings, and actions, you will have a greater understanding of how they affect the people around you. Because of your increased self-awareness, you are now able to better control your emotions, resolve disputes more skillfully, and communicate with more empathy and clarity.

Take into consideration a scenario in which a member of the team comes to you with a problem. You come to the conclusion, after engaging in some self-reflection, that when getting feedback, you have a propensity to become defensive. Armed with this knowledge, you have the ability to make the intentional decision to approach the dialogue with an open mind, carefully listening to the team member's viewpoint and reacting in a way that is more helpful. Because of this self-awareness and deliberate conduct, your team may experience better connections, greater collaboration, and more trust.

You are also able to establish significant objectives for yourself and devise a development strategy when you engage in self-reflection. SMART objectives are goals that are precise, measurable, attainable, relevant, and time-bound. You may construct SMART goals by selecting areas in which you would like to improve. You may think of your objectives as guideposts; they will provide direction and inspiration as you work toward achieving the results you seek.

Consider the following scenario: after giving some thought to your approach to leadership, you come to the conclusion that you want to improve your capacity to inspire and encourage the members of your team. You may use the SMART goal-setting technique to plan to attend leadership courses, study books on motivating leadership, and adopt new ways to engage and empower the people on your team. Reviewing and contemplating your progress toward these objectives on a regular basis paves the way for ongoing development and improvement.

It is essential to keep in mind that the act of self-reflection necessitates the allocation of specific time and space for introspection. This may be accomplished by participating in activities that increase self-awareness, such as going for walks in nature or practicing mindfulness, by engaging in practices such as journaling, meditation, or meditation, or by engaging in activities that enhance self-awareness. You can make self-reflection a habit and put your personal growth and development at the forefront of your mind by incorporating it into your daily routine.

When it comes to one's own growth and development as a manager, the act of regularly engaging in self-reflection is an extremely helpful tool. You may improve your self-awareness, acquire new insights into your strengths and limitations, connect your activities with your values, and create objectives for your own personal development by engaging in self-reflection. You may become a more successful and self-aware leader by participating in continual self-reflection. This will allow you to drive positive change and create success within your team and business. Therefore, make sure you give yourself enough time to stop, think, and put money into your professional development as a manager.

In summary, developing a growth mindset is essential for success as a manager. Embrace challenges, learn from failures, practice perseverance, develop a positive attitude towards change, and practice self-reflection. With a growth mindset, you can achieve your goals and reach your full potential.

The Mindful Manager

PART - III
MINDFUL
COMMUNICATION

In a vibrant urban center, there existed a conscientious and esteemed manager named Shivani. Shivani was known for her exceptional leadership skills, but she felt there was still room for improvement. She recognized that active listening was a crucial skill she needed to develop in order to enhance her effectiveness as a leader and create a more harmonious work environment for her team.

Shivani understood that active listening went beyond simply hearing words; it involved fully engaging with the speaker, understanding their perspective, and responding empathetically. Determined to cultivate this skill, she made a conscious effort to practice active listening in her daily interactions with her team members.

During team meetings, Shivani gave her undivided attention to each speaker, maintaining eye contact and refraining from interrupting. She asked open-ended questions to encourage her team members to express their thoughts and ideas more fully. By actively listening, she created an atmosphere where her team felt valued and empowered, leading to increased employee engagement and productivity.

One day, Shivani's team faced a challenging project. During a brainstorming session, one of her team members, Alex, shared an innovative idea. Shivani demonstrated her active listening skills by showing genuine interest, asking clarifying questions, and thanking Alex for their valuable contribution. Alex felt appreciated and motivated, knowing that their ideas were valued. This strengthened their confidence and the bond between Shivani and the team.

Active listening also helped Shivani build trust among her team members. By genuinely caring about their thoughts, ideas, and concerns, Shivani fostered an environment where her employees felt comfortable discussing both their successes and challenges. This trust enabled Shivani to tailor her leadership style to meet individual needs, ultimately enhancing job satisfaction and commitment within the team.

In another instance, Shivani had a one-on-one meeting with an employee named Emily. Emily expressed her dissatisfaction with her current role and sought more challenging opportunities. Shivani actively listened, giving her undivided attention, and refrained from making snap judgments. By understanding Emily's concerns, Shivani collaboratively explored different options for resolving the challenges Emily faced. This not only showcased Shivani's commitment to her employees' growth but also strengthened their relationship, leading to increased loyalty and dedication.

Furthermore, Shivani realized that active listening played a vital role in resolving disagreements within the team. By attentively listening to different perspectives and seeking areas of agreement, Shivani created an atmosphere of respect and collaboration. This approach increased the chances of finding solutions that satisfied everyone's needs, fostering a more positive and cohesive work environment.

By practicing active listening, Shivani also gained valuable information and diverse viewpoints. She understood that actively engaging with her team members' ideas, suggestions, and feedback allowed her to make well-informed decisions that considered multiple perspectives. This inclusive approach resulted in more effective leadership and successful outcomes for the team as a whole.

Inspired by her commitment to active listening, Shivani encouraged her team members to practice it as well. She provided them with tips and guidance on how to be attentive, ask relevant questions, reflect on others' perspectives, and respond appropriately. Together, they created a culture of active listening where open communication and mutual understanding thrived.

Through her dedication to active listening, Shivani transformed herself into a truly effective leader. Her team flourished under her guidance, trust, and collaboration increased, and the work environment became more enjoyable and productive for everyone involved.

Practical Examples:

1. During a team meeting, Shivani actively listened to each team member's suggestions for a new marketing campaign. She asked probing questions to better understand their ideas and provided feedback that showed she had truly absorbed their input. This led to a more collaborative and successful campaign.

2. Shivani had a one-on-one discussion with a team member, John, who was struggling with a project. Instead of dismissing his concerns, Shivani actively listened to John's challenges and offered support and guidance. By showing empathy and understanding, Shivani helped John overcome obstacles and regain his confidence.

3. In a performance review session, Shivani practiced active listening by attentively listening to an employee's self-assessment and feedback. She asked follow-up questions to delve deeper into the employee's perspective and collaboratively set goals for improvement. This empowered the employee and strengthened their trust in Shivani's leadership.

4. During a team conflict resolution meeting, Shivani facilitated active listening among the involved parties. She encouraged each team member to express their concerns while ensuring that everyone had an opportunity to be heard. Through active listening, Shivani helped the team find common ground and reach a mutually beneficial solution.

5. Shivani practiced active listening in her interactions with stakeholders outside her team. Whether it was a client, a supplier, or a senior executive, she focused on understanding their needs and concerns. This allowed her to build stronger relationships, negotiate more effectively, and find win-win solutions.

By implementing active listening in various scenarios, Shivani demonstrated the power of this skill in creating a positive and productive work environment, fostering collaboration, and building trust among team members.

CHAPTER 7
ACTIVE LISTENING

As a manager, the ability to be an active listener is a skill that is highly valuable and has the potential to have a big impact on both your effectiveness as a leader and the overall success of your team. Active listening is a talent that has the potential to have a major influence on both your efficiency as a leader and the overall success of your team. Active listening involves more than just hearing the words; it entails thoroughly engaging with the speaker, absorbing the information they are trying to convey, and responding in a way that demonstrates both empathy and comprehension. If you participate in active listening, you may increase your relationships with the other members of your team, build an environment of trust, and make your place of employment a more enjoyable place to be overall.

One of the key benefits of active listening is that it helps to create an environment that is safe and that encourages open and honest communication. This is one of the primary advantages of active listening. When employees have the perception that their ideas and views are really appreciated and heard by their superiors, they are more likely to speak up, express their perspectives, and contribute to the success of the team. This makes it easier for employees to contribute to the success of the team. By actively listening to what your employees have to say, you can foster an atmosphere in which they feel appreciated and empowered, which, in turn, can lead to increased levels of employee engagement and productivity.

Take into consideration the possibility that a member of your team may provide you with an original idea for one of your projects. To demonstrate that you are an active listener, you should give the other person your complete attention, maintain eye contact with them while they are speaking, and refrain from interrupting them or attempting to rush through the conversation. You would show appreciation for the member's input by asking open-ended questions to encourage them to expand on their idea, seeking clarification where required, and thanking them for their involvement in the discussion. You may be able to boost someone's self-assurance and motivation by actively listening to what they have to say and letting them know that their thoughts are valued in the context of this circumstance. This creates a scenario in which everyone engaged comes out ahead, so it's a win-win for everyone concerned.

One additional advantage of active listening is the development of trust among the members of your team. When employees think that their manager takes an honest interest in their thoughts, ideas, and concerns, they are more likely to have confidence in their own judgment, go to their manager for assistance when they need it, and feel comfortable discussing both their successes and their challenges. This is because when workers believe that their manager takes an honest interest in their thoughts, ideas, and worries, they are more likely to be really interested in those things. Active listening is one of the essential roles you can play in creating and maintaining trust among the members of your team. Trust is the foundation of constructive cooperation and collaboration, and active listening is one of the most important roles you can play.

In addition, engaging in active listening exercises helps you get a deeper grasp of the needs, goals, and motivations of the members of your team. You will be able to customize your leadership style to their individual remarks, issues, and career goals if you attentively listen to their feedback and concerns and then utilize that knowledge to deliver actual help and opportunities. This will allow you to tailor your leadership style to their specific comments, problems, and career aspirations. This customized approach not only helps to increase the satisfaction of workers but also contributes to the growth of a sense of loyalty and commitment to both the team and the company as a whole.

Take into account the likelihood that an employee may express their dissatisfaction with the role that they are now playing in the organization during a one-on-one meeting with the employee's supervisor. To be an active listener is to give the other person your undivided attention, to make an attempt to grasp the issues that they are facing, and to refrain from making any snap decisions or assuming anything about the context of the conversation. If you participate in active listening and pay attention to what the person says, it's probable that the employee is searching for employment that is more challenging or that has opportunities for promotion. You may demonstrate your commitment to the employee's professional development and strengthen the relationship between the employee and management by identifying the challenges faced by the employee and working together with the employee to investigate the many options available for resolving those challenges.

The ability to actively listen is also very important to the successful resolution of disagreements. When there are differences within a group, practicing active listening helps you to totally appreciate the points of view of all of the individuals affected, identify areas of agreement, and seek solutions that are helpful to all of the people involved. You may be able to build an atmosphere that is respectful of others and favorable to collaboration by carefully taking in the viewpoints of all parties involved. This, in turn, enhances the likelihood of finding a solution that satisfies the requirements of all parties concerned.

In addition, the skill of active listening may help you acquire important information and make well-informed judgments, so it's a good idea to work on developing it. If you pay close attention to the ideas, suggestions, and feedback provided by the other members of your team, you will have a better chance of acquiring access to helpful information as well as a variety of points of view. This information may serve to direct your decision-making process, providing you with the capacity to analyze a number of views and eventually lead to solutions that are both more successful and more inclusive.

If one wants to improve the talent of active listening, it is vital to put certain tactics into practice. Examples of excellent listening skills include maintaining eye contact, adopting open body language, avoiding interruptions, summarizing or paraphrasing what the speaker has said to ensure understanding, and asking questions that clarify topics. In addition, it is necessary not to be preoccupied with other ideas or distractions but rather to be entirely present at the moment and to take a true interest in what the speaker is saying rather than being distracted by other things. Instead of being fascinated by other ideas or distractions, it is best to pay full attention to what the speaker is saying.

Managers really need to be able to participate in active listening since it is one of the most important skills they may have. If you pay attention to what your coworkers have to say and make an effort to understand what they are saying, you may foster a positive culture at work, increase trust among your employees, and facilitate open communication with them all. You are able to gain a deeper awareness of the needs, motivations, and objectives of your employees by practicing active listening, which, in the end, results in more effective leadership, stronger cooperation, and increased employee engagement. You should make it a top priority as a manager to participate in active listening so that both you and your team may take advantage of the many benefits that this management technique provides. These benefits are for everyone involved.

Here are some tips for practicing active listening:

1. **Pay attention:** When someone is speaking, give them your full attention. Put away any distractions and focus solely on what they are saying.

2. **Ask questions:** Encourage the speaker to elaborate on their thoughts and feelings by asking open-ended questions. This shows that you are engaged and interested in what they have to say.

3. **Reflect:** Paraphrase what the speaker is saying to ensure that you understand their message accurately. This also shows that you are actively listening and care about their perspective.

4. **Empathize:** Put yourself in the speaker's shoes and try to see things from their point of view. This helps build trust and shows that you value their feelings and opinions.

5. **Respond appropriately:** Once the speaker has finished, respond in a way that shows that you have understood their message. This could be by summarizing their points, expressing empathy, or offering advice or support.

Active listening is especially important in high-pressure environments, where communication breakdowns can lead to misunderstandings and conflict. By practicing active listening, managers can create a more productive and collaborative workplace culture.

Moreover, active listening can help managers identify and resolve problems before they escalate. By listening to employees' concerns, managers can take proactive steps to address issues and prevent them from becoming more significant.

CHAPTER 8
EMPATHY AND COMPASSION

Empathy and compassion are two important traits that every manager should possess. In today's fast-paced business environment, it is easy to get caught up in the daily grind and forget about the human element of management. However, it is important to remember that the people who work for you are not just cogs in a machine but human beings with their own needs, desires, and struggles.

Empathy is the ability to understand and share the feelings of another person. As a manager, it is important to be able to put yourself in your employees' shoes and understand their perspectives. This can be particularly challenging if you are in a position of power and authority, but it is essential if you want to create a positive and productive work environment.

One way to cultivate empathy is by actively listening to your employees. Make an effort to hear their concerns and feedback, and respond with understanding and empathy. This can go a long way in building trust and fostering a culture of open communication.

Compassion, on the other hand, is the willingness to take action to alleviate the suffering of others. As a manager, it is important to not only understand your employees' struggles but to take steps to address them. This might involve offering support and resources, such as counseling or flexible work arrangements, or simply showing kindness and understanding.

Compassion can also extend beyond your employees to your customers, suppliers, and other stakeholders. By putting yourself in their shoes and understanding their needs and challenges, you can build stronger relationships and create a more sustainable and successful business.

Empathy and compassion are essential traits for any manager who wants to create a positive and productive work environment. By cultivating these qualities and putting them into practice, you can build stronger relationships with your employees and stakeholders and ultimately achieve greater success in your business.

CHAPTER 9
EFFECTIVE FEEDBACK

As a manager, one of the most important things you can do for your team is to provide them with effective feedback. Feedback is a crucial tool for promoting growth, development, and overall success. However, it can be challenging to deliver feedback in a way that is both constructive and well-received. The following tips can help you provide feedback that will be beneficial to both you and your team.

1. Be specific: The more specific your feedback is, the more helpful it will be. Instead of saying, "Great job," try saying, "I appreciate the way you handled that difficult customer. Your calm demeanor and clear communication skills helped to resolve the issue quickly and effectively." This type of feedback not only acknowledges the employee's efforts but also provides specific examples of what they did well.

2. Focus on behavior, not personality: When giving feedback, it's essential to focus on the employee's behavior and actions rather than their personality or character. For example, instead of saying, "You're lazy," say, "I've noticed that you've been missing deadlines and not completing tasks on time. How can we work together to improve your productivity?"

3. Use the "sandwich" approach: The "sandwich" approach is a common technique used to deliver feedback. It involves starting with a positive comment, followed by constructive feedback, and ending with another positive comment. This approach can help soften the blow of criticism and make it easier for the employee to hear and accept the feedback.

4. Avoid criticism: Criticism can be demotivating and unproductive, so it's essential to avoid it whenever possible. Instead of criticizing, try framing your feedback in a positive way. For example, instead of saying, "You made a mistake," say, "Let's work together to find a solution to this challenge."

5. Make it timely: Feedback is most effective when it is given in a timely manner. Don't wait until the end of the year or a performance review to provide feedback. Instead, give feedback as soon as possible after the event or behavior you are addressing. This will help the employee understand the impact of their actions and make changes more quickly.

Providing effective feedback is an essential part of being a successful manager. By following these tips, you can provide feedback that is specific, behavior-focused, positive, and timely, which will help your team grow and succeed.

PART - IV
TIME MANAGEMENT AND PRIORITIZATION

The Mindful Manager

In a fast-paced corporate environment, there was a dedicated and ambitious manager named Mark. Mark was known for his exceptional time management skills, but he knew that identifying priorities was crucial to achieving success in his high-pressure role. He understood that without proper prioritization, he risked losing track of important tasks, missing deadlines, and experiencing unnecessary stress.

To tackle this challenge, Mark developed a systematic approach to identifying priorities. He began by clearly defining his goals and objectives. By understanding what he wanted to achieve, he could align his tasks with the overarching vision and focus on activities that directly contributed to his desired outcomes.

Next, Mark assessed the urgency and importance of each task. He categorized them based on their level of immediacy and their impact on his long-term goals. This allowed him to differentiate between tasks that required immediate attention and those that could be deferred. By prioritizing urgent and important tasks, Mark ensured that he remained on track and consistently made progress toward his objectives.

Understanding his resources and constraints was also essential for Mark when identifying priorities. He evaluated his available skills, expertise, and time to determine whether he could handle certain tasks effectively or if he needed to delegate them or seek additional support. By making informed decisions based on his available resources, Mark optimized his efficiency and effectiveness in managing his workload.

Mark recognized the importance of effective communication with his team. He regularly communicated his priorities to ensure that everyone was aligned and understood the urgency and significance of each task. By providing clear guidance and empowering his team members to take action, Mark fostered a collaborative work environment where everyone worked towards shared goals, even when he was occupied with other priorities.

Flexibility and adaptability were key attributes that Mark embraced in his approach to identifying priorities. He understood that unexpected challenges and changing circumstances were inevitable in a high-pressure environment. Therefore, he remained agile and willing to adjust his priorities when necessary. By staying mindful of his goals and objectives, he could make well-informed decisions and maintain focus amidst shifting demands.

Mark's commitment to identifying priorities paid off in numerous ways. He consistently met deadlines, delivered high-quality work, and achieved his goals. His effective time management skills not only reduce stress and burnout but also inspired his team to adopt similar practices. Together, they created a culture of productivity and success.

Practical Examples:

1. When faced with a sudden client request, Mark assessed its urgency and importance relative to his ongoing projects. He communicated with his team, reprioritized tasks, and allocated resources accordingly, ensuring the client's needs were met while minimizing the impact on existing commitments.

2. During a busy period with multiple simultaneous projects, Mark used the Pomodoro technique to manage his time effectively. He broke down his work into focused intervals, dedicating each Pomodoro to a specific task. This allowed him to maintain concentration and make progress on various projects without feeling overwhelmed.

3. Mark's team member approached him with a personal issue that required immediate attention. Recognizing the urgency and the well-being of his team member, Mark reprioritized his tasks and provided the necessary support. By demonstrating empathy and understanding, he built trust and strengthened the bond within his team.

4. As a manager, Mark regularly conducted performance reviews with his team members. During these meetings, he actively listened to their career aspirations, assessed their strengths and weaknesses, and collaboratively set development goals. By prioritizing their growth and aligning it with the team's objectives, Mark nurtured a motivated and engaged workforce.

5.   Mark used his time management skills to allocate sufficient time for strategic thinking and long-term planning. By dedicating specific time blocks to reflect on the broader vision and identify future priorities, he ensured that his decisions aligned with the company's objectives and anticipated future challenges.

Through Mark's dedication to identifying priorities and effectively managing his time, he not only excelled in his role as a manager but also inspired his team to optimize their productivity and achieve their goals. His commitment to balancing urgency, importance, resources, and flexibility served as a valuable lesson for others navigating high-pressure environments.

CHAPTER 10
IDENTIFYING PRIORITIES

Identifying priorities is a critical skill for any manager in a high-pressure environment. With a never-ending list of tasks and responsibilities, it can be challenging to figure out what requires immediate attention and what can wait. However, if you don't prioritize your tasks, you risk missing deadlines, making mistakes, and, ultimately, failing to achieve your goals.

To identify your priorities, you need to start by understanding your goals and objectives. What are you trying to achieve? What are the key outcomes you are working towards? Once you have a clear understanding of your objectives, you can start breaking them down into smaller, more manageable tasks.

Next, you need to assess the urgency and importance of each task. Urgent tasks require immediate attention, while important tasks contribute to your long-term goals. Ideally, you want to focus on tasks that are both urgent and important, but sometimes you may need to prioritize one over the other.

It's also essential to consider your resources and constraints when identifying your priorities. Do you have the necessary skills and expertise to complete a particular task? Do you have the time and resources to devote to it? If not, you may need to delegate the task or seek additional support.

As a manager, it's crucial to communicate your priorities with your team. By doing so, you can ensure that everyone is working towards the same goals and that they understand the urgency and importance of each task. Additionally, you can empower your team to make decisions and take action when you're unavailable or focused on other priorities.

Finally, it's essential to be flexible and adaptable when identifying your priorities. A high-pressure environment can be unpredictable, and you may need to shift your focus and reprioritize tasks based on changing circumstances. By staying mindful and aware of your goals and objectives, you can make informed decisions and stay on track toward achieving success.

Identifying priorities is a critical skill for any manager in a high-pressure environment. By understanding your goals and objectives, assessing the urgency and importance of each task, considering your resources and constraints, communicating with your team, and being flexible and adaptable, you can effectively manage your workload and achieve success.

CHAPTER 11
SETTING REALISTIC GOALS

Setting realistic goals is an essential part of being a successful manager. As a manager, you are responsible for not just your own goals but also the goals of your team. It is important to set realistic goals that are achievable and measurable. In this subchapter, we will explore the benefits of setting realistic goals and how to set them effectively.

CHAPTER 12
BENEFITS OF SETTING REALISTIC GOALS

Setting realistic goals can have several benefits for managers. Firstly, it can help increase motivation and productivity. When goals are achievable, it gives employees a sense of accomplishment which can motivate them to work harder. Secondly, it can help reduce stress and anxiety. Unrealistic goals can create unnecessary pressure and stress, which can result in burnout. Lastly, setting realistic goals can improve communication and collaboration. When goals are clear and achievable, it creates a sense of shared purpose and encourages teamwork.

CHAPTER 13
TIPS FOR SETTING REALISTIC GOALS

1. **Define clear objectives** - Start by defining clear objectives for yourself and your team. Make sure these objectives are specific, measurable, achievable, relevant, and time-bound (SMART).

2. **Break down larger goals -** Break down larger goals into smaller, more manageable tasks. This will make it easier to track progress and identify areas that need improvement.

3.   **Involve your team -** Involve your team in the goal-setting process. This will give them a sense of ownership and motivate them to work towards achieving the goals.

4.   **Prioritize goals -** Prioritize goals based on their importance and urgency. This will help you and your team focus on the most important tasks first.

5.   **Review and adjust goals -** Review goals regularly and adjust them if necessary. This will ensure that goals remain relevant and achievable.

Setting realistic goals is an essential part of being a successful manager. It can help increase motivation and productivity, reduce stress and anxiety, and improve communication and collaboration. By following these tips, managers can set effective goals that are achievable and measurable.

CHAPTER 14
THE POMODORO TECHNIQUE

The Pomodoro technique is a time management method developed by Francesco Cirillo in the 1980s. The technique is named after the tomato-shaped kitchen timer that Cirillo used to time his work intervals. The Pomodoro technique is designed to help individuals manage their time more efficiently by breaking work down into focused intervals.

The Pomodoro technique involves dividing your workday into 25-minute intervals, known as Pomodoros. During each Pomodoro, you work on a single task without interruption. After each Pomodoro, you take a short break of three to five minutes. After four Pomodoros, you take a longer break of 15 to 30 minutes.

The Pomodoro technique is based on the idea that by breaking your work down into focused intervals, you can improve your concentration and productivity. It also helps you to avoid distractions and procrastination, as you are only focusing on a single task during each Pomodoro.

As a manager, the Pomodoro technique can be a great tool to help you manage your workload more effectively. By using the technique, you can prioritize your tasks and ensure that you are making progress on your most important projects. It also helps you to avoid burnout by taking regular breaks throughout the day.

Workers, owners, and manufacturers can also benefit from the Pomodoro technique. It can help workers to stay focused on their tasks and complete them more efficiently. Owners can use the technique to manage their time more effectively and ensure that they are making progress on their projects. Manufacturers can use the technique to streamline their production processes and increase their output.

Overall, the Pomodoro technique is a simple but effective time management method that can help individuals to manage their workload more efficiently. By breaking work down into focused intervals, you can improve your concentration, productivity, and overall well-being. As a manager, it is important to encourage your team to use the technique and support them in their efforts to manage their time more effectively.

PART - V
STRESS MANAGEMENT AND "WORK-LIFE BALANCE"

In a thriving corporate setting, there existed a manager named Shivani, where the hustle and bustle of the office filled the air. Shivani was known for her dedication and hard work, but the demanding nature of her role often led to stress and overwhelming pressure. Recognizing the importance of managing stress, both for herself and her team, Shivani made it a priority to develop effective coping mechanisms.

Shivani understood that stress could impact anyone in the workplace, regardless of their position. She took the time to educate herself on the signs of stress, such as physical symptoms like fatigue and headaches, emotional symptoms like anxiety and irritability, and behavioral symptoms like changes in eating habits or social withdrawal. By recognizing these signs, Shivani could intervene early and address the underlying causes of stress before it escalated into burnout or other negative consequences.

To manage her own stress, Shivani embraced mindfulness techniques, particularly mindful breathing and meditation. She set aside a few minutes each day to find a calm and quiet space where she could focus on her breath and bring her attention to the present moment. This practice allowed her to cultivate inner calm, stay centered, and maintain focus even in high-pressure situations. Shivani also encouraged her team members to adopt mindfulness practices, leading by example and creating a supportive environment that prioritized well-being.

In addition to mindfulness, Shivani understood the importance of physical exercise in reducing the detrimental effects of stress. She encouraged her team to engage in regular exercise routines, emphasizing the release of endorphins and the positive impact on mental and emotional well-being. Shivani herself made time for exercise, whether it was a brisk walk during lunch breaks or attending fitness classes after work. She noticed that regular exercise not only boosted her own resilience but also created positive energy within the team.

Shivani recognized that personal pursuits and hobbies were crucial for stress management. She encouraged her team members to make time for activities they enjoyed, whether it was reading, playing a musical instrument, pursuing creative endeavors, or spending quality time with loved ones. By prioritizing these activities, Shivani knew that her team members could find a sense of joy and relaxation outside of work, allowing them to recharge and maintain a healthy work-life balance.

As a manager, Shivani emphasized the importance of self-care. She encouraged her team to prioritize their mental, emotional, and physical well-being. Shivani led by example, ensuring she obtained sufficient restful sleep, consumed nourishing foods, and took regular breaks to prevent exhaustion. She emphasized that seeking professional help from a mental health specialist was not a sign of weakness but a proactive step to take care of one's mental health.

Through her dedication to stress management, Shivani became a resilient, productive, and fulfilled manager. Her team members admired her ability to handle stress and appreciated the supportive environment she created. Shivani's example inspired others to develop healthy coping mechanisms, leading to a happier and more productive workplace overall.

Practical Examples:

1. Shivani noticed that one of her team members, Alex, seemed fatigued and irritable. She recognized these as signs of stress and approached Alex in a compassionate manner. After a conversation, Shivani adjusted Alex's workload and provided resources for stress management, such as recommending mindfulness apps and suggesting exercise breaks during the workday.

2. During a particularly stressful project, Shivani noticed that the team's morale was declining. She decided to introduce a mindfulness session at the beginning of team meetings, where everyone could take a few minutes to practice mindful breathing together. This helped to center the team and create a calmer and more focused atmosphere.

3. Shivani organized a team-building activity centered around hobbies and personal interests. She encouraged each team member to share their hobbies and provided dedicated time during the workweek for them to engage in these activities. This fostered a sense of connection, relaxation, and renewed energy within the team.

4. Shivani recognized that one of her team members, Emily, was consistently working late and neglecting self-care. She

approached Emily and discussed the importance of setting boundaries and prioritizing personal well-being. Together, they created a schedule that allowed Emily to dedicate time for exercise, hobbies, and self-care routines, resulting in increased overall happiness and improved job performance.

5. Shivani regularly shared articles, books, and resources related to stress management and well-being with her team. She encouraged open discussions about stress and implemented a "stress-free zone" in the office where employees could take short breaks, practice deep breathing, or engage in quick mindfulness exercises whenever needed.

These practical examples illustrate how Shivani's commitment to stress management positively influenced her team and created a supportive work environment that prioritized well-being and productivity.

CHAPTER 15
RECOGNIZING SIGNS OF STRESS

Stress is a common experience in the workplace, and it can affect anyone, regardless of their position or job title. As a manager, it is important to recognize the signs of stress in yourself and your team members, as this can help you to address the issue before it leads to burnout or other negative consequences.

The signs of stress can vary from person to person, but some common indicators include:

1. **Physical symptoms:** Fatigue, headaches, muscle tension, and stomach problems are all physical symptoms that can be caused by stress.

2. **Emotional symptoms:** Anxiety, irritability, and depression are all emotional symptoms that can be caused by stress.

3. **Behavioral symptoms:** Changes in eating or sleeping habits, increased alcohol or drug use, and social withdrawal are all behavioral symptoms that can be caused by stress.

If you notice any of these signs in yourself or your team members, it is important to take action to address the underlying causes of stress. This may involve making changes to work schedules or workloads, providing training or support to help employees manage stress, or encouraging employees to seek professional help if necessary.

As a manager, it is also important to lead by example and model healthy stress management habits. This includes taking breaks throughout the day, setting realistic goals, and practicing mindfulness and other stress-reduction techniques.

By recognizing the signs of stress and taking proactive steps to address them, you can help to create a healthier and more productive workplace for yourself and your team members.

CHAPTER 16
COPING MECHANISMS FOR STRESS

Dealing with the unavoidable obligations and expectations that come along with one's position as a manager is one of the most difficult parts of holding a managerial position. The obligation of being responsible for the achievements of a group or organization might, at times, seem like an impossible load to those who have accepted it. In spite of this, you don't have to let stress determine how you spend the rest of your life. By putting helpful coping skills into practice, you may learn to handle stress and prevent burnout, and as a consequence, you may ultimately become a more resilient and content manager.

The practice of mindfulness is a helpful tool for overcoming challenging circumstances. Mindfulness is a technique that involves paying attention to one's interior experiences and evaluating one's thoughts and feelings without making any judgments about what one finds there. Because of this capacity, even when the stakes are really high, you will be able to keep a sense of calm and remain focused on the task at hand. When it comes to incorporating mindfulness into your day-to-day activities, you have a wide variety of various options to choose from. One example of this is the practice of meditation, which involves setting aside a certain period of time each day to engage in introspection and discover a sense of inner serenity. When you're under a lot of pressure, it might be helpful to practice deep breathing so that you can bring yourself back to the center. Another way to cultivate a sense of awareness is to disconnect from one's technological gadgets for a brief period of time and direct one's attention to the world that is immediately around them.

Exercising regularly is yet another helpful method for reducing the detrimental effects of stress. Endorphins are naturally occurring chemicals in the body that have the effect of lifting one's mood. When you exercise, your body produces more endorphins. A regular exercise program not only has a beneficial influence on your physical health, but it also has a favorable effect on both your mental and emotional state. If you exercise regularly, you may reap the benefits of all three. It is possible that engaging in even brief bouts of physical activity on a daily basis might have a significant impact on one's ability to manage stress and overall level of happiness.

When you're trying to balance many responsibilities at once, it's tempting to let your personal pursuits and hobbies go by the wayside. Nevertheless, making time for fun activities is one of the most essential components of good stress management. Hobbies provide a form of creative expression in addition to serving as a means of relaxation for the person who engages in them. As a consequence of this, you are able to create some space between yourself and the pressures of your job and restock both your mental and emotional resources. Put the things that bring you joy and provide you the opportunity to get back into your hobbies at the top of your to-do list. Activities like reading a book, playing a musical instrument, pursuing creative efforts, and spending quality time with loved ones are examples of these types of activities.

In addition to engaging in mindfulness techniques, engaging in physical exercise, and maintaining interests, effective stress management also demands consistently engaging in self-care routines. When it comes to practicing self-care, one of the most crucial aspects is making sure that your mental, emotional, and physical wellness comes first. A sufficient quantity of restful sleep, the consumption of nourishing foods, and taking regular pauses are all important aspects of self-care. If you obtain the amount of restorative sleep that you need each night, you will wake up feeling more refreshed and more able to cope with the effects of stress. If you give your body meals that are rich in nutrients, it will be able to provide you with the power and vitality you need in order to meet the challenges of daily life. By pausing whenever it is necessary, you may prevent yourself from being exhausted and give yourself the opportunity to recharge. It is vital to bear in mind that seeking help from a mental health professional is not a sign of weakness but rather a step that is proactive in nature and serves to take care of one's mental health. If you feel that the consequences of stress or other worries linked to your mental health are becoming too much for you to take, do not be afraid to seek the support of a professional specialist who can help you through this difficult time.

Developing good coping skills is one of the most essential things you can do as a manager to manage stress and prevent burnout. This is one of the most important things you can do. If you include self-care into your daily routine and incorporate things like exercise, hobbies, and mindfulness meditation, you may be able to effectively manage stress and maintain your wellness. Putting your own health and happiness ahead of the needs of the team and the business as a whole is not only helpful for you as an individual, but it also has a significant effect on the organization as a whole. By demonstrating how to successfully deal with stress in a positive manner, you may inspire others in your immediate environment to cultivate healthy coping methods and establish a supportive environment at your place of employment. You will become a manager who is more resilient, productive, and fulfilled in their job if you use these tactics for coping with difficult circumstances.

CHAPTER 17
MINDFUL BREATHING AND MEDITATION

It is essential for managers, employees, owners, and manufacturers in today's contemporary workplace to prioritize their personal well-being and develop effective stress management strategies in order to thrive in spite of the hectic and demanding nature of the modern workplace. Individuals are able to attain inner peace and maintain a good work-life balance by incorporating strong practices such as mindful breathing and meditation into their day-to-day routines.

The process of practicing mindful breathing may serve as a basic technique for developing a condition that is characterized by tranquillity and concentration. A person may access the present moment and enjoy a variety of advantages just by focusing their attention on the breath as it moves naturally in and out of the body. In contrast to other techniques, mindful breathing may be performed at any location and at any time and does not call for the use of specialized equipment or formal instruction.

To begin the practice of mindful breathing, it is necessary to choose a calm location with few distractions since this is a prerequisite for the exercise. First, ensure that you are in a comfortable sitting posture with your back straight and your hands resting on your lap. Next, shut your eyes slowly and deliberately while taking several deep breaths. Then, bring one's whole attention to the act of breathing in and out. Become aware of the feelings that occur when air travels through the body, first entering the nose, then filling the lungs, and finally exiting the body. In the event that the mind wanders, bring it back to the breath in a gentle manner in order to restore awareness of the here and now.

Meditation, an additional powerful method, may further increase one's awareness as well as their sense of inner calm. Individuals may enjoy the advantages of decreased stress, greater well-being, and increased attention by deliberately setting out time for quiet contemplation and using that time in the appropriate manner. During meditation, one's attention is often focused on a particular object, such as the breath, a mantra, or a vision. The mind is able to relax, and one has a greater sense of calm as a result of this concentrated concentration.

Find a calm location with few distractions in order to start a meditation practice, and dress comfortably and quietly. Assume a comfortable sitting posture, making that the spine is straight and the hands are resting lightly on the lap. Close your eyes and direct your attention to your breathing while you do so. In a manner similar to that of mindful breathing, anytime the mind wanders, gently bring it back to focusing on the breath. Alternately, one may imagine a calm and pleasant landscape, quietly repeat a mantra, or focus their attention on a particular area of the body.

In a nutshell, the consistent practice of mindful breathing and meditation enables people to successfully manage stress and nurture general well-being in the workplace. Managers, employees, owners, and manufacturers may all build inner tranquility by devoting a few minutes each day to these routines. This enables them to negotiate high-pressure circumstances with better clarity and composure.

Meditation and mindful breathing both have advantages that reach beyond the individual practitioner. When managers start using these techniques, they are setting an example for their team members and helping to cultivate a culture at work that places emphasis on employees' well-being and promotes stress management. Recharging their batteries and regaining their concentration are both possible outcomes for employees who put these strategies to use during downtime or in high-pressure circumstances. It is possible for owners and manufacturers to cultivate settings that place a priority on the mental and emotional well-being of their personnel. This, in turn, will result in higher productivity and general contentment in one's work.

It is beneficial for managers, employees, owners, and manufacturers to include meditation and mindful breathing in their daily life. There are several benefits to doing so. These practices give the skills that are necessary to properly manage stress, develop inner calm, and maintain a good work-life balance. Individuals are able to improve their general well-being and become more resilient and productive on the job by devoting a small amount of time each day to these activities that have the potential to impact their lives.

PART - VI
MINDFUL LEADERSHIP

In a lively corporate environment, there resided a manager by the name of Mark, where the constant activity of the office permeated the atmosphere. Mark believed in the power of leading by example and understood the significant impact it could have on his team and the overall work culture. With a genuine desire to create a positive and collaborative environment, Mark embarked on a journey to foster teamwork, open communication, and personal growth within his team.

Mark started by cultivating awareness of his own actions and behaviors. He practiced mindfulness, dedicating moments each day to be fully present in the here and now. This allowed him to lead with undivided focus, ensuring he was attentive to his team's needs and concerns. By demonstrating mindfulness, Mark set an example for his team, encouraging them to find meaning and purpose in their work and make conscious decisions that aligned with the values and work ethic he desired from them.

Communication was another crucial element for Mark in leading by example. He believed in open and honest communication, creating an environment where his team felt comfortable expressing their thoughts and ideas. Mark actively listened during team meetings, valuing the concerns and suggestions voiced by his employees. Through effective communication, he fostered trust and respect within the team, setting a positive example that encouraged his employees to communicate openly with one another. This, in turn, improved teamwork, problem-solving, and overall productivity.

Accountability was a core value for Mark, and he made sure to lead by example in this aspect as well. He took complete responsibility for his actions, decisions, and mistakes, never shying away from acknowledging his shortcomings. By demonstrating responsible conduct, Mark became a role model for his team, creating a culture that emphasized ownership and learning from mistakes. His transparency cultivated trust among employees, empowering them to take ownership of their work and strive for continuous improvement.

Mark understood that leading by example required consistent effort and dedication. He regularly reflected on his own behavior, seeking areas where he could grow and progress professionally. Mark actively sought feedback from his team members and remained open to constructive criticism. By exemplifying a commitment to personal and professional development, he inspired his team to do the same, fostering a culture of continuous learning and advancement.

Mark's efforts to lead by example resulted in a positive work culture where employees felt valued, respected, and supported. His team members admired his behavior and emulated his positive and respectful demeanor. The atmosphere became one of collaboration and camaraderie, with employees motivated to work hard and achieve their goals. Mark's commitment to leading by example transformed him into a powerful agent of change, boosting productivity, expanding possibilities for cooperation, and creating a work environment that celebrated accomplishments.

Practical Examples:

1. Mark noticed that his team members were hesitant to speak up during meetings. He took the initiative to actively listen and encourage open communication. During meetings, Mark started by expressing his own thoughts and ideas, creating a safe space for others to contribute. Over time, his team members followed suit, and the meetings became more engaging and productive.

2. One of Mark's team members, Shivani, made a mistake that affected a project's timeline. Instead of blaming Shivani, Mark accepted responsibility for not providing clear instructions. He discussed the issue openly with the team, emphasizing the importance of accountability and learning from mistakes. This set an example for the entire team, fostering a culture of responsibility and continuous improvement.

3. Mark organized regular team-building activities outside of work hours to foster a sense of community. He encouraged his team members to participate in volunteer events or engage in shared hobbies and interests. These activities helped build stronger relationships among team members, enhancing collaboration and creating a positive work environment.

4. Recognizing the importance of personal growth, Mark encouraged his team members to attend conferences, workshops, and training programs. He actively supported their professional development by providing resources and opportunities for skill enhancement. Mark's own dedication to continuous learning inspired his team members to explore new avenues and take on new challenges.

5. Mark implemented a flexible work policy that allowed employees to have a better work-life balance. He understood that productivity could be influenced by personal well-being. By allowing flexible work hours and remote work options, Mark demonstrated his commitment to supporting his team's overall happiness and mental well-being.

These practical examples illustrate how Mark's dedication to leading by example transformed the work culture within his team. Through mindfulness, effective communication, accountability, personal growth, and creating a positive work environment, Mark paved the way for his team's success and fostered a thriving, collaborative atmosphere.

CHAPTER 18
LEADING BY EXAMPLE

The concept that a manager can influence the performance of their team and the overall mood of the workplace by setting a good example for their subordinates is more than just platitude; it is an effective management approach. The idea is that a manager can influence the performance of their team and the general ambiance of the workplace by setting a good example for their subordinates. When managers completely commit to the concept that they should lead by example, they convert into agents of positive change. As a result, they motivate their workforce to perform at the greatest possible level and cultivate an atmosphere that rewards accomplishments. When managers pay attention to their activities, cultivate excellent communication skills, and accept responsibility for their acts, they have the capacity to pave the path for the success of their firm.

Managers need to begin by cultivating awareness in their own actions and behaviors in order to effectively set an example for others to follow. The act of paying attention to the here and now with undivided focus, without allowing ideas or actions from the past or future to enter one's consciousness, is what the practice of mindfulness implies. If they make mindfulness a regular part of their life, managers may give their staff a sense of meaning and purpose in the work they do. They are able to make conscious judgments to serve as a model for the values and work ethic they require from their personnel because they get a deeper knowledge of how the things they do affect people around them. Mindful managers inspire the people of their teams to mimic their behavior via a range of behaviors. These acts include actively listening during team meetings and demonstrating a devotion to quality in their own work.

Engaging in good communication is another crucial element that must be present for leading by example to be successful. Managers who are able to communicate in a manner that is not just open and honest but also very clear are more likely to cultivate an environment at work that is based on trust and respect. They make an effort to hear the concerns and ideas voiced by their employees, which in turn helps those employees feel heard and valued in the workplace. When managers demonstrate to their staff how to communicate effectively, they not only improve teamwork and relationships but also create a more pleasant working atmosphere. This is because they are setting a positive example for their employees. When there are no glitches in the communication process, there is a considerable improvement in both the problem-solving and production processes.

It is critical for managers to demonstrate the importance of accountability by being responsible for their own actions. Accepting complete responsibility for one's actions, decisions, and erroneous judgments is a necessary component of it. When managers demonstrate responsible conduct by holding themselves accountable, they not only serve as role models for the members of their team, but they also contribute to the development of a culture that places a premium on responsibility. Instead of laying blame on others or giving excuses, accountable managers acknowledge their own shortcomings, take the lessons they've gained from those shortcomings, and try to improve their performance. This kind of transparency helps to cultivate trust among employees and encourages them to take ownership of the job that they do, which, in the end, leads to higher productivity and a heightened sense of agency throughout the team.

In order to be a positive role model for other people, you can't just do something once; rather, it takes consistent effort and dedication over time. It is expected of managers that they are willing to consistently reflect on their own behavior, searching for areas in which they may evolve and progress professionally. This is a requirement that managers must meet. They should make it a practice to regularly get feedback from the members of their team and remain receptive to accepting useful criticism. Additionally, they should make it a priority to gather feedback.

By exemplifying a commitment to their own personal and professional development, managers can show their teams that advancement is an ongoing process and inspire their employees to do the same. The message that this conveys to workers is that they are not excluded from the path of development. This sensitivity contributes to the development of a culture of ongoing learning and advancement, which, in turn, pushes individuals to take risks and examine new avenues of possibility.

One of the fundamental tenets of management is to act as a model for others to emulate, and every manager should subscribe to this attitude. It is feasible for managers to establish a pleasant environment at work in which people feel inspired, respected, and empowered if they participate in mindful practices, communicate effectively, and accept ownership of their actions. In this scenario, employees will feel encouraged to work hard and accomplish their goals. When managers behave in the ways they hope their people will, they morph into powerful agents of change who boost productivity, expand possibilities for cooperation, and cultivate an atmosphere that rewards accomplishments. To lead by example is not only about saying the right things; rather, it is about doing things that have a long-lasting effect on the overall performance and welfare of the complete team. Keep this in mind. Leading by example is not just about saying the right things.

CHAPTER 19
CREATING A POSITIVE WORK CULTURE

As a manager, you play a crucial role in creating a positive work culture. A positive work culture is one where employees feel valued, respected, and supported. When employees feel happy and engaged at work, they are more productive, and the company benefits as a whole. Here are some tips for creating a positive work culture:

1. **Lead by example:** As a manager, your behavior sets the tone for the rest of the team. Lead by example and show your employees how to behave in a positive and respectful manner.

2. **Recognize and reward good work:** Employees want to feel valued and appreciated. Make sure to recognize good work and reward employees for their efforts.

3. **Encourage open communication:** Create an environment where employees feel comfortable sharing their thoughts and ideas. Encourage open communication and listen to feedback from your team.

4. **Foster a sense of community:** Encourage team-building activities and create opportunities for employees to get to know each other outside of work. This can help foster a sense of community and teamwork.

5. **Provide opportunities for growth:** Employees want to feel like they are growing and developing professionally. Provide opportunities for training and development, and encourage employees to take on new challenges.

6. **Be flexible:** Create a flexible work environment where employees can balance work and personal life. This can include flexible work hours, remote work options, and other benefits that support work-life balance.

Creating a positive work culture takes time and effort, but the benefits are well worth it. By creating a positive work environment, you can improve employee morale, increase productivity, and ultimately drive business success. As a manager, it's your responsibility to lead the way and create a work culture that supports your team.

CHAPTER 20
FOSTERING TEAMWORK AND COLLABORATION

Fostering teamwork and collaboration is essential for any organization to achieve its goals. In today's fast-paced, high-pressure work environment, it is even more crucial to have a team that can work together effectively and efficiently.

As a manager, you have a vital role to play in building a culture of collaboration and teamwork. Your team members look up to you for guidance, support, and direction. You need to lead by example and demonstrate the importance of working together towards a common goal.

Here are some tips for fostering teamwork and collaboration:

1. **Encourage open communication:** Create an environment where team members feel comfortable sharing their thoughts and ideas. Encourage them to speak up and express their opinions. Listen actively and provide feedback that is constructive and supportive.

2. **Build trust:** Trust is the foundation of any successful team. As a manager, you need to earn the trust of your team members by being honest, transparent, and reliable. Trust is built over time, so be patient and consistent in your actions.

3. **Set clear goals and expectations:** Make sure that everyone on the team understands what they are working towards and what is expected of them. Be specific and provide clear guidelines and deadlines.

4. **Celebrate successes:** Recognize and celebrate the achievements of your team members. This helps to build morale and encourages everyone to work harder towards the next goal.

5. **Foster a culture of collaboration:** Encourage team members to work together and collaborate on projects. Provide opportunities for cross-functional teams to work together on projects that require diverse skills and perspectives.

6. **Provide training and development opportunities:** Invest in the professional development of your team members. This helps to build their skills and knowledge and also shows that you care about their growth and development.

By following these tips, you can foster a culture of teamwork and collaboration that will help your organization thrive in today's high-pressure work environment. Remember, as a manager, you have the power to lead by example and create a positive work environment that brings out the best in your team members.

PART - VII
MINDFUL DECISION-MAKING

Once in a bygone era, within a bustling corporate office, a manager by the name of Shivani held her position. Shivani was a thoughtful and open-minded leader who understood the importance of identifying biases, making data-driven decisions, and balancing intuition and logic in her role. She believed that by embracing these principles, she could create a harmonious and successful work environment for her team.

Shivani recognized that biases exist within everyone, including herself, and that they could impact decision-making and relationships within the workplace. She made a conscious effort to identify and overcome her biases by engaging in self-reflection and seeking input from her team members. Shivani encouraged open and honest dialogues, creating an inclusive atmosphere where diverse perspectives were valued and respected.

To make informed decisions, Shivani emphasized the importance of data-driven approaches. She understood that relying solely on intuition or personal experience could lead to biases and potential errors. Shivani implemented systems to collect and analyze relevant data, enabling her to identify trends, mitigate risks, and streamline operations. By leveraging data, she made well-informed decisions that positively impacted the team's performance and overall business goals.

Shivani also recognized the value of balancing intuition and logic. She understood that intuition could provide valuable insights, particularly in understanding and managing her team's emotions and motivations. However, she knew the importance of complementing intuition with logical reasoning and data-driven evidence to ensure the best outcomes for the company and its employees. Shivani actively involved her team in the decision-making process, seeking their input and diverse perspectives to strike the right balance between intuition and logic.

Practical Examples:

1. Shivani noticed that she had a slight preference for promoting team members who shared similar backgrounds or communication styles as her own. To address this bias, she implemented a structured evaluation process that focused on objective criteria such as performance, skills, and potential. By relying on data and removing personal biases, Shivani ensured fair opportunities for growth and advancement within her team.

2. In a brainstorming session, Shivani observed that one team member, Alex, was hesitant to share their ideas. Sensing their discomfort, Shivani used her intuition to approach Alex privately, creating a safe space for them to express themselves. By balancing intuition and empathy with logical reasoning, Shivani discovered that Alex was concerned about their ideas being dismissed. She reassured

Alex and encouraged them to share their thoughts openly, fostering a culture of inclusivity and collaboration.

3. When faced with a critical business decision, Shivani sought input from her team members, who possessed different expertise and perspectives. By involving them in the decision-making process, Shivani leveraged their collective wisdom and knowledge. This approach helped her uncover blind spots, evaluate alternatives, and arrive at well-rounded decisions that considered multiple viewpoints.

4. Shivani implemented diversity and inclusion programs within the workplace, including unconscious bias training and inclusive recruitment practices. By embracing data-driven insights on the benefits of diverse teams, Shivani promoted an environment that celebrated different backgrounds and perspectives. This not only enhanced employee engagement but also led to increased innovation and creativity.

5. Recognizing the importance of work-life balance, Shivani used data on employee productivity, satisfaction, and well-being to implement flexible work policies. By considering both logical data and the well-being of her team members, Shivani struck a balance that allowed individuals to thrive both personally and professionally.

These practical examples demonstrate how Shivani's commitment to identifying biases, making data-driven decisions, and balancing intuition and logic positively influenced her leadership and the overall work environment.

Her dedication to creating an inclusive, informed, and harmonious workplace enabled her team to reach their full potential and achieve remarkable success.

CHAPTER 21
IDENTIFYING BIASES

As humans, we all have biases. Biases are the unconscious attitudes or beliefs that we have about certain groups of people or situations. Biases can affect our decision-making, communication, and relationships with others. As a manager, it is crucial to be aware of your biases and how they may impact your team and workplace.

The subtle and often unconscious impacts on our thoughts and choices that are known as biases may have a major impact on both our perceptions and our behaviors. These cognitive shortcuts may lead us astray and impede our capacity to make fair and objective judgments. Some examples of cognitive shortcuts are confirmation bias, anchoring bias, and availability prejudice. Nevertheless, we may become more aware managers and cultivate inclusive working environments if we acknowledge and try to overcome the prejudices that we have.

Confirmation bias is one of the most common types of prejudice, and it refers to our natural tendency to look for data that corroborates our preexisting opinions while ignoring evidence that runs counter to those beliefs. This alluring fallacy has the potential to distort our judgment and hinder us from taking into account alternate points of view. It is essential to develop a mentality of intellectual curiosity and open-mindedness if one wants to combat this kind of prejudice. Seek knowledge that both questions the validity of your views and stimulates your capacity for critical thought. Take part in civil arguments and conversations with the members of your team in order to cultivate an atmosphere that is open to a variety of points of view.

Another prevalent kind of prejudice that may trip up managers is known as the anchoring bias. When we do this, we put a disproportionate amount of weight on the very first piece of information that comes our way, which might result in erroneous judgments on our part. Before making a final choice, you should make it a point to obtain information from a variety of sources and give thought to contrasting points of view in order to eliminate any potential for prejudice. Encourage everyone on your team to share their unique perspectives and to question the original assumptions made. You may liberate yourself from the anchoring bias and make decisions that are more informed and nuanced if you extend the knowledge source you draw from.

When managers make choices based only on the information that is easily accessible to them, they are susceptible to availability bias because they fail to take into account a more comprehensive set of facts. The ease with which one may retrieve information from memory or the effect of recent events is often the cause of this bias. Develop a habit of making decisions based on the facts you have available to you in order to combat the availability bias. Encourage your team to give exhaustive data and do an analysis of the complete spectrum of the information that is currently accessible. The use of organized decision-making procedures that incorporate systematic assessment may assist in mitigating the effects of this bias.

It is necessary to engage in self-reflection and introspection in order to determine our own personal biases. Spend some time reflecting on your own experiences and the things you believe. Put to the test any preconceived notions you may have about certain categories of individuals or certain kinds of circumstances. Have open and honest dialogues with yourself, and look for input from people you trust, such as coworkers or mentors. Their points of view have the potential to enlighten you about prejudices that you may not be aware of and to assist you in expanding your awareness.

As soon as you've recognized your own prejudices, you may start working to lessen the damage they do. Actively seeking out the thoughts and experiences of people from a wide range of backgrounds is one of the most successful tactics. Encourage the members of your team to share their opinions and ideas, even if they go against what you have in mind. Create a welcoming atmosphere in which people from all walks of life may freely express their opinions without worrying that they will be judged or ignored without exception. Develop connections with people who come from a variety of different life experiences and make it a point to actively interact with people from different backgrounds.

In the workplace, implementing diversity and inclusion programs may also assist in building an atmosphere that celebrates and respects differences in people's perspectives and experiences. Unconscious bias education programs, diverse recruiting practices, and inclusive policies are all examples of the kind of activities that fall under this category. Your staff will get a crystal clear message that their ideas and talents are appreciated, regardless of their background, if you make a conscious effort to promote diversity and inclusion in the workplace.

The process of being aware of one's own prejudices and attempting to lessen the damage they do is a continuous one. It is necessary to have self-awareness, humility, and a dedication to personal development. You may make your workplace more welcoming and effective by addressing the prejudices that exist there. You create an atmosphere in which people feel appreciated for who they are and what they bring to the table, where decisions are made in a fair and impartial manner, and where creativity is allowed to flourish.

Keep in mind that prejudices are an inevitable aspect of the human condition. Recognizing the existence of one's own inherent biases is essential, given that everyone does so to some extent. The way in which we confront and actively attempt to reduce our prejudices is, however, the aspect that is most important. We can become more conscious managers who can inspire and encourage our staff to attain their full potential if we accept the challenge of overcoming prejudices and make it one of our own personal goals to do so.

CHAPTER 22
THE IMPORTANCE OF DATA-DRIVEN DECISIONS

In today's fast-paced business environment, making informed decisions is critical to the success of any organization. As a manager, it is your responsibility to ensure that your decisions are based on accurate and reliable data. In this subchapter, we will discuss the importance of data-driven decisions and how they can help you achieve your business goals.

Data-driven decisions are those that are based on data analysis and interpretation. This means that you use data to understand the current state of your business, identify trends, and make informed decisions that will improve your operations. By leveraging data, you can gain insights that would be impossible to obtain through intuition or experience alone.

One of the primary benefits of data-driven decisions is that they help you to mitigate risks. When you rely on data, you can identify potential issues before they become major problems. For example, if you notice a trend of declining sales in a particular region, you can investigate the cause of the decline and take corrective action before it affects your bottom line.

Another advantage of data-driven decisions is that they can save you time and money. By using data to identify inefficiencies in your operations, you can streamline your processes and reduce costs. For example, if you notice that your employees are spending a significant amount of time on administrative tasks, you can implement automation tools that will free up their time for more valuable activities.

Data-driven decisions also help you to remain competitive in your industry. As markets become more saturated and customer demands evolve, it is critical to stay ahead of the curve. By using data to understand your customer's needs and preferences, you can develop products and services that meet their expectations and differentiate yourself from your competitors.

Data-driven decisions are essential for any manager looking to succeed in today's business environment. By leveraging data, you can mitigate risks, save time and money, remain competitive, and achieve your business goals. As a mindful manager, it is your responsibility to ensure that your decisions are based on accurate and reliable data.

CHAPTER 23
BALANCING INTUITION AND LOGIC

In any professional setting, it's essential to strike a balance between intuition and logic. While intuition can help you make quick decisions, logic ensures that you make the right choice. As a manager, you need to learn how to use both to your advantage.

Intuition is a powerful tool that can help you make decisions quickly, especially when you're under pressure. However, it can also lead to impulsive decisions that are not always right. Therefore, it's important to evaluate your intuition before making any decisions.

One way to balance intuition and logic is to gather as much information as possible before making a decision. This means taking the time to research and collect data that will help you make an informed decision. Once you have all the facts, you can use your intuition to make a quick decision.

Another way to balance intuition and logic is to involve others in the decision-making process. This can help you get different perspectives and ideas that you may not have considered before. It also helps to have a team of people who can support your decisions and provide feedback.

When it comes to managing people, intuition can be especially useful. As a manager, you need to be able to read people and understand their emotions and motivations. This can help you create a positive and productive work environment. However, you also need to use logic to ensure that you're making decisions that are in the best interest of the company and its employees.

Balancing intuition and logic is essential for any manager. It's important to use both to your advantage, taking the time to gather information and involve others in the decision-making process. With practice and experience, you can learn to strike the right balance between intuition and logic and become a more effective manager.

PART - VIII
MINDFUL PRODUCTIVITY

In a vibrant city, there existed a manager named Shivani, who was known for her unwavering dedication and tireless work ethic. Shivani was known for her exceptional organizational skills and her ability to handle multiple projects simultaneously. She was always determined to meet deadlines and ensure the success of her team. However, Shivani often found herself feeling overwhelmed by the constant distractions and demands of her role.

One day, Shivani realized that she needed to find a way to regain her focus and improve her productivity. She embarked on a journey to discover effective methods to eliminate distractions and enhance her ability to concentrate. She read books, attended workshops, and sought advice from successful managers who had mastered the art of staying focused in a chaotic work environment.

With newfound knowledge and determination, Shivani implemented various strategies to eliminate distractions from her work environment. She created a dedicated workspace, free from unnecessary interruptions, by closing her office door and using noise-canceling headphones. She also set specific times to check emails and limited her access to social media during work hours.

Shivani learned the importance of prioritizing tasks and creating a detailed plan to accomplish them within specific timeframes. By breaking down larger projects into smaller, manageable tasks, she increased her attention span and felt a sense of accomplishment as she progressed through her workload.

Recognizing the value of regular breaks, Shivani incorporated short moments of relaxation and mindfulness into her daily routine. She practiced deep breathing exercises, went for walks, and engaged in meditation during her breaks. These rejuvenating moments allowed her mind to rest and refocus, leading to increased productivity and creativity.

As Shivani embraced these strategies and made them a part of her daily routine, she experienced a significant improvement in her ability to concentrate. She became a role model for her team, demonstrating the power of eliminating distractions and finding focus in a fast-paced work environment.

Practical Example:

Let's take the example of Mark, a manager in a software development company. Mark was known for his exceptional technical skills, but he often struggled to maintain focus due to constant distractions. He realized that in order to lead his team effectively and deliver high-quality projects, he needed to find a way to eliminate distractions and improve his attention span.

Following the advice in the given content, Mark took proactive steps to eliminate distractions from his work environment. He allocated specific blocks of time during the day to check and respond to emails, avoiding the constant interruptions caused by incoming messages. Mark also implemented website blocking tools to limit his access to social media and other distracting websites while he was working on important tasks.

To create a conducive working environment, Mark started using noise-canceling headphones to block out background noise and interruptions in the office. He also encouraged his team members to respect each other's need for uninterrupted focus by implementing a "quiet time" policy during certain periods of the day.

Recognizing the importance of regular breaks, Mark incorporated short intervals of relaxation and mindfulness into his daily schedule. During these breaks, he practiced deep breathing exercises and took short walks to clear his mind and recharge. As a result, he found that he was able to maintain his focus for longer periods and approach his work with renewed energy and creativity.

Mark's improved ability to eliminate distractions and find focus had a positive impact on his productivity and the overall performance of his team. By setting an example and encouraging his team members to adopt similar strategies, they were able to accomplish more in less time and achieve better results.

Mark's journey to find focus and eliminate distractions demonstrates the practical application of the strategies outlined in the given content. By implementing these techniques, he was able to enhance his attention span, prioritize tasks effectively, create a conducive work environment, and improve overall productivity.

Sandeep Roy | 148

CHAPTER 24
FINDING FOCUS

In the hectic and fast-paced world of management, the ability to keep one's focus is more than just important; it is absolutely essential. There is a chance that your progress may be thwarted, and as a consequence, you may find yourself feeling overwhelmed as a result of this. There are diversions lurking around every corner. However, there is no need for you to freak out since there are effective methods at your disposal that you can use to restore your attention and stay on track in spite of the chaos that is taking place.

In order to get started, getting rid of distractions is one of the most crucial things you can do since it will have the biggest impact on the situation. This requires you to first detect the extraneous influences that are pulling your attention away from the job at hand and then actively make efforts to decrease the effect of those forces. In order to do this, you must first acknowledge the influences, and then you must actively take action. You may find it helpful to shut the door to your office when you need to concentrate on work so that there is a physical barrier between you and anybody who could disturb you. You should either put your phone on silent mode or turn it off entirely if you don't want to give in to the enticing pull of notifications. When you are meant to be working, you have the ability to block access to certain websites or limit the amount of time you spend on social media. You may create an environment that is favorable to focus, and that allows you to totally submerge yourself in the task at hand if you make a concentrated effort to reduce the number of distractions that you are exposed to. This will allow you to establish an atmosphere that is conducive to concentration and that enables you to completely immerse yourself in the work at hand.

Clearly defining your goals and laying out a plan to accomplish them within a certain amount of time is another productive strategy for improving your attention. When you have a firm understanding of the actions that need to be carried out, as well as the time frame within which they must be completed, you will be in a better position to prioritize the activities that you engage in and more successfully manage your time. Instead of attempting to multitask or giving in to the desire to put things off until later, you have the choice of prioritizing your workload and doing one item at a time instead of giving in to the temptation to put things off until later. By dividing larger tasks into smaller, more manageable chunks, you might potentially boost your attention span as well as your sense of making progress and accomplishing things as you go through more difficult projects.

It can seem counterintuitive, but taking breaks at predetermined times throughout the day is a fantastic way to improve attention while also increasing total productivity. It's a common myth that working longer hours and straining oneself more strenuously in order to attain better outcomes is the path to success. This is a mistake. The findings of a number of studies have revealed that pausing often may, in fact, boost cognitive performance and foster more creative thinking. Taking a break from your work, even if it's only for a few minutes, provides your brain with the opportunity to rest, rejuvenate, and redirect its resources. Make the most of these brief moments to stretch, go for a walk, or engage in any kind of meditation that focuses on being attentive. If you take care of your health and allow your mind some time to rest, you'll find that you can go back to your work with a renewed sense of vigor and an increased ability to concentrate on what's important.

When we speak about being mindful, we imply that by including activities such as meditation and deep breathing exercises in your daily routine, you may be able to do wonders for both your ability to focus and your stress levels. By committing a part of each day to the practice of mindfulness activities, such as slowing the mind and focusing on the flow of breath, you may be able to dramatically increase your ability to be present in the here and now as well as retain your center. This may result in a major improvement in your ability to stay centered. By engaging in activities that cultivate mindfulness, you may clear your mind of the mental clutter that hinders your ability to focus and hone in on the task at hand. You will, as time goes on, develop more resilience, emotional intelligence, and mental clarity, all of which will make it easier for you to navigate the challenges and hurdles that come up in both your professional and personal lives.

The capacity to find one's focus and maintain it is a talent that is essential not only for managers and workers but also for owners and manufacturers. You may be able to enhance your ability to concentrate and complete what you have set out to achieve if you make a deliberate effort to eliminate any possible distractions, clarify your goals in detail, plan regular breaks, and participate in activities that build mindfulness. If you are prepared to commit yourself and stay persistent, you can cultivate the focus and resilience you need to thrive in the high-pressure world of today. Therefore, in order for your level of productivity to reach new heights, you will need to recover your attention, uncover your entire potential, and allow yourself to fully realize all of your capabilities.

CHAPTER 25
ELIMINATING DISTRACTIONS

It is all too easy to get entangled in the web of distractions that surround us in today's fast-paced world of management. Because of this, it could be difficult to keep one's attention on the job at hand. Our email inboxes are overflowing, our colleagues are vying for our attention, and our own thoughts are meandering aimlessly. In the midst of everything going on, it may seem like an uphill battle to maintain one's attention and level of productivity at a high level. On the other side, removing distractions is not only necessary for attaining success, but it is also the first step toward being a mindful manager.

The first step in getting rid of distractions is to identify the source of the problem that caused them in the first place. Is it the repetitive beeping that occurs every time you get a notification on your smartphone? Is the incessant small talk going on in the background amongst coworkers? It's also possible that the way your mind wanders is what leads you to lose focus on the task at hand and get distracted. After you have isolated the sources of distraction in your working environment, you will be in a position to make concerted attempts to eliminate those distractions after you have figured out where they are coming from.

An effective strategy for reducing the detrimental impacts of distractions is to devise a schedule that sets out certain times throughout the day for the completion of a variety of tasks. For example, if you find that constantly checking and responding to emails throughout the day pulls your attention away from the core activities you need to do, you should set certain blocks of time during which you will interact with your email account. If you do this, you will be able to concentrate on a single task at a time, which will allow you to steer clear of the constant interruptions caused by an unending stream of email notifications.

Creating a working environment that is free of possible distractions is another excellent method for lowering the number of interruptions that occur during work. You may want to consider closing the door to your place of business as a hint that you need some time to concentrate in peace. You might, as an alternative, invest in headphones that have noise-canceling technology in order to drown out the ambient noise in the working environment. In addition, make use of productivity tools such as website blocks, which restrict your access to potentially distracting websites during the hours that you have set aside for work. This will help you get more done in the time that you have set aside.

It is also extremely important to make sure that you give both your body and mind plenty of opportunities to unwind and revitalize themselves by pausing often. According to the findings of a number of different studies, taking a few brief breaks during the workday may, in fact, enhance productivity while also preventing burnout. Take a little break from what you're doing and engage in an activity that will help you unwind and clear your head, such as going for a short walk, giving meditation a try, or engaging in some exercises that focus on deep breathing. Because they provide you with a much-needed respite from the constant flow of stimuli, you will be able to return to your task with renewed attention and excitement after taking one of these pauses. This is because these breaks offer you a break from the constant stream of stimulus.

Now, let's take a look at a scenario that demonstrates the benefits of reducing distractions from your environment:

Alex is a manager who is determined and thinks ahead of the curve, and under his direction, the squad constantly performs at a high level. As a result of Alex's awareness of the detrimental impact that possible sources of distraction have on productivity, he has made it one of his primary goals to eliminate any potential sources of distraction from the workplace. Alex begins each day by doing an assessment of his surroundings to look for any potential interruptions. He then takes proactive measures to remedy any problems he discovers.

One of the many things that may easily distract Alex's attention is the never-ending stream of email notifications. This is only one of the numerous things. Alex counteracts this by allocating certain blocks of time in the morning, throughout lunch, and in the afternoon to check and respond to his emails. By focusing only on his email during the allotted times, Alex is able to avoid giving in to the urge to check his inbox at random intervals and instead maintain a healthy level of self-control. As a direct consequence of this, he is in a better position to concentrate on various other tasks that are very important.

Alex is often distracted by the chaotic environment of the office, which is characterized by a lot of loud sounds and frequent interruptions. In response to this, Alex has implemented a "closed-door" policy at certain periods of the day or week when it is essential for him to focus his attention very intently on his work. By shutting the door to his office, Alex is letting his employees know that they need uninterrupted time to focus on their projects. In addition, Alex is able to maintain his flow state and make the most of his productivity by utilizing noise-canceling headphones, which are extremely beneficial in decreasing distractions in the background. This allows Alex to make the most of his time spent working.

Alex ensures that he takes regular, short breaks throughout the day in order to reduce the amount of mental exhaustion he experiences and keep his productivity at its highest potential level. During these times, Alex will engage in activities that help him become more conscious, such as meditation or exercises that include deep breathing. These few moments of respite provide a precious opportunity to revitalize oneself and refocus one's attention, both of which, in the long term, will lead to higher-quality work output.

Eliminating distractions is one of the most crucial elements of evolving into a mindful manager, and it's also one of the most critical tasks. You will be able to develop concentration, improve productivity, and negotiate the high-pressure demands of your profession with clarity and calmness if you identify the sources of distraction, schedule particular times for activities, create a work environment that is free of distractions, and take frequent breaks. By taking a strategic approach to managing distractions at work and actually putting that strategy into action, you can increase the likelihood of reaching your full potential and succeeding in today's highly competitive work environment.

CHAPTER 26
THE POWER OF DELEGATION

As a manager, you are well aware of the weight of responsibility that comes with managing the work of your team, ensuring that the project is successful, and addressing any challenges that may arise. You can easily feel overworked and fatigued due to the sheer quantity of duties that you are accountable for, which might easily lead you to feel that way. On the other hand, delegation is a powerful tool that you have at your disposal, and it has the potential to aid in relieving some of the stress and freeing up important time for you.

Delegation refers to the process of passing on tasks and duties to other members of your team who are responsible for them. It makes it possible for you to draw on the expertise and experience of the other people in your team, which in turn makes it possible for you to do a greater quantity of work in a shorter length of time. Not only will this result in an improvement in your own personal productivity, but it will also provide the other members of your team with greater autonomy and more opportunities to acquire new skills.

One of the key advantages that come with delegating work is the increased ability to focus on the obligations that are considered to be the most important. As a manager, one of the essential things you do is pick the route that your team will pursue, and you also need to make sure that the organization as a whole is moving in the right direction. You make it feasible for yourself to devote more of your time and mental capacity to higher-level tasks such as strategic planning and decision-making, both of which are vital to attaining long-term success when you delegate duties to other members of your team. This makes it possible for you to achieve your long-term goals more quickly.

In addition to this, delegation serves as a catalyst for creating trust among the members of your team and fostering cooperation among them. When you delegate tasks to other people, you demonstrate that you have trust in the capacity of the other members of your team to carry out the job at hand in an efficient manner. This act of trust helps establish a feeling of ownership and responsibility among the members of your team, which eventually results in increased performance as well as a stronger sense of unity amongst the members of your group.

Despite this, the process of distributing tasks is not always straightforward and simple to grasp. It is not always easy to let go of control and trust that the members of your team will carry out their responsibilities to the standard of excellence that you anticipate. Nevertheless, it is vital to understand that delegation is a process that involves a journey and requires clear communication, guidance, and ongoing support. This acknowledgment is required since delegation is a process that involves a trip. You have a duty to provide the members of your team with the information, resources, and authority they need, in addition to making yourself available to provide feedback and coaching that will aid them in growing their skills.

For the purpose of gaining a deeper comprehension of the significance of effective delegation, let's examine the following fictitious scenario:

Imagine that you're a manager by the name of Alex and that you're in charge of an energetic crew that works in a chaotic environment. You are well aware of the fact that you have a lot of responsibilities, and as a consequence, you examine the skills and attributes of the individuals that make up your team. You give them duties that are appropriate for their level of expertise, their areas of interest, and the areas in which you want them to develop professionally. If you do this, you will not only decrease the amount of work that you need to do, but you will also give the members of your team a chance to grow professionally and demonstrate their skills. If you do this, you will reduce the amount of work that you have to accomplish.

For instance, you decide to entrust Emma, who is well-known for her meticulousness and attention to detail, with the task of finishing a challenging research project. Because of this assignment, Emma will have the chance to further hone her research skills and show that she is capable of accurately evaluating facts. Not only will you be putting Emma's talents to good use, but you will also be proving that you believe in her capabilities by acting in this manner.

Because John is such a productive and well-organized member of the team, you make the executive decision to hand over to him the responsibility of planning the project schedules. By entrusting John with the completion of this assignment, you are enabling him to further develop the natural capacity he has for planning and coordination. This not only makes your job simpler, but it also provides John with the opportunity to take on a greater degree of responsibility for the manner in which the project is progressing.

In addition to this, effective delegation may assist in the development of a culture of collaboration and shared responsibility within the group that you are responsible for managing. When members of a team are assigned responsibility for certain tasks, they start to feel responsible for the team as a whole and the work that they have accomplished. When people understand the significance of the contributions they make, they are more likely to get interested, inspired, and ready to put forth their best effort.

Making smart use of delegation, which is a powerful tool, may help you boost the productivity of your team while also fostering an environment of trust and cooperation among its members and enhancing the individual capabilities of those individuals. It is necessary for a manager to master the art of delegation and make efficient use of it in order to maintain a solid work-life balance while working in high-pressure settings. This will allow the manager to better balance their professional and personal lives. Not only will you be able to cut down on the amount of work you have to do by effectively delegating tasks and responsibilities to other members of your team, but you will also be able to offer them more authority and push them to reach even higher levels of success with their efforts. It is important to keep in mind that effective delegation is both an investment in the growth of your team and a means toward the attainment of group goals. Keep this in mind while you delegate tasks.

PART - IX
MINDFUL WORK-LIFE BALANCE

4

In a bustling city, there resided a manager named Emily, as the urban landscape buzzed with activity all around. She worked for a highly demanding company where the pressure was always on. Emily was dedicated to her job and strived for success, but she often found herself overwhelmed and struggling to maintain a healthy work-life balance.

One day, during a particularly stressful period, Emily attended a workshop on mindfulness in the workplace. She learned about the importance of setting boundaries, prioritizing self-care, and nurturing personal relationships. The workshop opened her eyes to new perspectives and strategies that could help her navigate the challenges she faced.

Inspired by what she had learned, Emily decided to take a proactive approach to setting boundaries. She identified her priorities, both personally and professionally, and established clear limits to protect them. She started by carving out dedicated time for her family, making sure she was fully present during those moments. Emily also learned to say no when necessary, realizing that she couldn't take on every request without compromising her well-being.

To incorporate self-care into her routine, Emily began prioritizing activities that promoted her mental, emotional, and physical well-being. She set aside time each day for meditation and exercise, which helped her relax and recharge. Additionally, she made it a point to take breaks during the workday, allowing herself to step away from her desk and engage in rejuvenating activities.

Emily understood the importance of effective communication in setting boundaries and promoting self-care. She started having open and honest conversations with her colleagues and employees, clearly expressing her expectations and needs. By doing so, she created a supportive environment where everyone's well-being was valued, leading to increased productivity and job satisfaction.

As Emily continued to practice mindfulness, she realized the significance of nurturing personal relationships. She made quality time with her loved ones a top priority, setting boundaries around her work schedule to ensure she had dedicated moments for connection and bonding. Emily actively listened to her family and friends, giving them her undivided attention and making them feel heard and valued.

Through her efforts, Emily experienced a positive transformation. She found a better balance between work and personal life, reduced her stress levels, and improved her overall well-being. Not only did she benefit from these changes, but her team also thrived in the supportive work environment she had fostered.

Practical Examples:

1. Laura, a manager in a high-pressure corporate environment, identified that spending time with her children was a top priority. To set boundaries, she made it

a rule to turn off work-related notifications during family time, allowing her to be fully present and engaged with her kids.

2. Michael, a team leader in a fast-paced startup, recognized the importance of self-care. He started incorporating short meditation breaks into the workday, encouraging his team members to join him. These brief moments of mindfulness helped reduce stress and improve focus, leading to increased productivity.

3. Shivani, a manager in a customer service department, understood the significance of personal connections. She organized team-building activities outside of work, such as volunteer events or social outings, to strengthen the bond among her team members. This not only enhanced their working relationships but also created a sense of camaraderie and support.

The journey of Emily and the practical examples demonstrate the importance of mindfulness in the workplace. By setting boundaries, prioritizing self-care, and nurturing personal relationships, managers can create a healthier work-life balance, improve their well-being, and foster a positive environment for their teams. Mindfulness is not just a buzzword but a practical approach that can lead to both personal and professional growth.

CHAPTER 27
SETTING BOUNDARIES

One of the biggest challenges that managers face in their personal and professional lives is setting boundaries. This is especially true for those who work in high-pressure environments where demands are constantly coming in from every direction. In order to maintain a healthy work-life balance, it's crucial to establish clear boundaries that allow you to focus on your priorities without getting overwhelmed.

The first step in setting boundaries is to identify your priorities. What are the most important things in your life, both personally and professionally? Once you've identified these priorities, you can begin to set boundaries that protect them.

For example, if spending time with your family is a top priority, you may need to set limits on how much time you spend working outside of normal business hours.

Another key aspect of setting boundaries is learning to say no. It's natural to want to be helpful and accommodating, but saying yes to every request can quickly lead to burnout. If you're feeling overwhelmed, it's okay to politely decline a request or delegate it to someone else. Remember that your time and energy are valuable resources, and it's important to protect them.

In addition to saying no, it's also important to communicate your boundaries clearly and assertively. This may involve having difficult conversations with colleagues or employees, but it's essential to establish expectations and avoid misunderstandings. Be specific about what you can and can't do, and don't be afraid to ask for support when you need it.

Finally, remember that setting boundaries is an ongoing process. As your priorities and circumstances change, you may need to adjust your boundaries accordingly. Stay mindful of your needs and be willing to make changes as necessary to maintain a healthy work-life balance.

Setting boundaries is a crucial skill for managers in high-pressure environments. By identifying your priorities, learning to say no, communicating clearly, and staying mindful, you can establish boundaries that protect your well-being and allow you to focus on what matters most.

CHAPTER 28
PRIORITIZING SELF-CARE

There is a widespread misunderstanding that the key to being successful in the area of management is to put in a lot of long hours at work and push one's talents to their ultimate limit. This is a frequent mistake. Nevertheless, this misconception disregards an important component, which is the act of providing for one's own self-care needs. Not only is making self-care a priority necessary for one's personal well-being, but it also plays a critical role in one's capacity to become and stay a successful manager. Not only is it essential to make self-care a priority, but it's also essential to make it a priority. In this chapter, we will delve into the relevance of engaging in self-care practices and investigate some useful recommendations for implementing these practices into your day-to-day routines.

The term "self-care" refers to the actions that we consciously carry out in order to take care of our mental, emotional, and physical well-being. It is essential for managers to put a high focus on self-care if they want to have a healthy balance between their professional and personal lives. The practice of self-care encompasses a wide range of pursuits, including but not limited to engaging in strenuous physical exercise, practicing meditation, spending quality time with loved ones, and taking several breaks during the course of one's workday.

Making time for oneself to concentrate on one's own health and well-being is one of the most challenging difficulties that managers have to deal with. Taking care of oneself, on the other hand, is not a luxury purchase but rather a need that must be satisfied at all costs, and this fact must be acknowledged. One of the most effective strategies for managers to reduce their stress levels, increase their productivity, and enhance their overall feeling of job satisfaction is to practice self-care.

Before beginning the process of elevating self-care to a greater priority, managers should first conduct an assessment of their current level of work-life balance to determine where they stand personally. Think about the amount of time you spend on activities related to work in contrast to the amount of time you spend on things that are more meaningful to you on a personal level. This examination will provide useful insights, and it will also give you a chance to set goals for incorporating self-care strategies into your day-to-day activities.

Putting appropriate limits in place is another crucial step in the process of elevating one's own self-care to the position of top priority. It is the responsibility of the management of a firm to establish set working hours and prohibit employees from bringing work-related duties home with them. It is possible to achieve a healthy work-life balance by doing so, which will prevent burnout and allow for personal rejuvenation. Doing so will make it feasible.

In addition to defining clear limits for themselves, managers must make it a point to communicate with their employees the importance they place on self-care and the measures they take to meet those needs. In order to accomplish this goal, it may be necessary to break for lunch at predetermined times over the course of the workday, divide up responsibilities, and set fair deadlines. The open communication of these needs enables managers to develop a supportive atmosphere at work that places importance on the well-being of workers in addition to their productivity. This tactic is useful not just for the boss but also for the wellness and productivity of the team as a whole.

Imagine the following scenario in which a manager places a high focus on attending to his or her own well-being:

Alex is a manager who puts in a lot of effort and is passionate about his job. He knows how important it is for people to take care of themselves. After doing an evaluation of their efforts to strike a healthy balance between their professional and personal lives, Alex makes the decision to make it a top priority to include in their day-to-day routine activities that foster self-care. They begin by scheduling certain amounts of time into each day to dedicate to engaging in physical exercise, cultivating a contemplative practice, and spending meaningful time with loved ones. In addition to this, Alex sets clear limits for himself, ensuring that he leaves work-related tasks at the office and makes the most of his personal time by resting, renewing, and relaxing. He does this by establishing clear boundaries for himself. Alex is also skilled at conveying to the team their need for self-care, promoting breaks at various points during the workday, and creating a healthy environment in the workplace.

Because Alex is so committed to taking care of himself, they have seen a major change in him as a direct result of this. They feel a release from the stress that has been building up inside of them, which allows them to face the work at hand with renewed vigor and focus. Productivity and general job satisfaction are getting closer and closer to reaching new pinnacles of excellence. Alex is not the only member of the team to benefit from the advantageous modifications; rather, the whole squad enjoys the benefits afforded by the manager's comprehensive strategy. When members of a team are part of a team that has a supportive work environment that places a high focus on the well-being of its workers, those members report feeling more inspired, energized, and engaged in their work. This is especially true when the team in question places a high emphasis on the well-being of its employees.

It is not a frivolous luxury but rather a necessary component for managers who are serious about establishing a healthy work-life balance to make self-care their top priority. This is not because self-care is a frivolous luxury but rather because it is an essential component. Simply defining clear boundaries for oneself and including activities that promote self-care in one's daily routine may be an effective strategy for preventing burnout, increasing productivity, and boosting feelings of overall job satisfaction. It is important to keep in mind that taking care of oneself is not an act of selfishness but rather a crucial component for success in one's professional endeavors. Embrace the idea of self-care, and you'll quickly see how it can transform not just your personal life but also your professional one.

CHAPTER 29
NURTURING PERSONAL RELATIONSHIPS

It is easy, while juggling all of the responsibilities that come with being a manager, to lose sight of how important personal connections are. Nevertheless, maintaining these connections is essential not just for maintaining a good work-life balance but also for lowering levels of stress and improving general well-being. Consequently, let's investigate the art of cultivating personal connections and investigate new approaches to forging stronger ties between individuals.

Personal connections should always come first since they are of the utmost importance. Your position as a manager might be stressful at times, but it is important to ensure that you set aside time each week to spend with your loved ones and close friends. In order to make room for cultivating personal ties, it is important to establish boundaries around your work schedule and learn how to decline some business obligations. Keep in mind that work will always be there, but the time you spend with the people you care about the most is irreplaceable.

Next, one must never undervalue the significance of attentive listening. When you are spending time with the people you care about, give your undivided attention to them and listen attentively to what they have to say. Put away any distractions, such as your phone or thoughts relating to work, and give your whole attention to the topic at hand. You may show that you are attentive, validate their emotions, and develop a better foundation for successful connections by carefully listening to what the other person has to say.

Participating in activities with the people you care about might be an excellent way to forge stronger bonds with them. Discover common interests, go on exciting excursions, or just focus on making the most of the time you have together. These activities, like going for a hike across the countryside, preparing a meal in the same kitchen, or playing board games, all contribute to the formation of long-lasting memories and deeper bonds. The trick is to discover things that not only make everyone happy but also give them the opportunity to unwind and take pleasure in each other's company.

In addition, communication that is both open and honest is the oxygen that keeps personal connections alive. Share your thoughts, emotions, and requirements with the people you care about, and urge them to do the same. Because effective communication entails both speaking and listening, it's important to be attentive to the other person's ideas and worries. If you want to make sure that everyone remains connected, you might think about setting up frequent check-ins with your partner or other members of your family. This designated period enables open communication and contributes to the resolution of any problems or concerns before they become more difficult to manage.

You may build your connections and improve your general well-being by placing a higher priority on personal relationships, actively listening to others, participating in activities that you and others share, and cultivating open and honest communication. Let's picture a situation in which a manager decides to put these nurturing methods into effect.

Get to know Shivani, a manager who understands the need to maintain personal connections. She makes her family a top priority by scheduling regular nights off work so that she may spend quality time with her husband and their children. During these set-apart hours, she puts her job aside, has meaningful talks with her family members, and pays close attention to what they have to say about how they are feeling. In addition, Shivani organizes group activities for them to participate in, such as going to the park on the weekend so that they may get to know one another better, have a good time, and make treasured memories together. In addition, Shivani makes it a priority to maintain open lines of communication with the people who are important to her, ensuring that she and those people often engage in candid conversations about any difficulties or successes they may be facing.

The quality of Shivani's personal connections has improved as a direct consequence of her efforts. She notes a more balanced work-life dynamic, lower stress levels, and increased well-being for herself as well as her family as a result of her efforts. The fact that Shivani is so dedicated to maintaining healthy personal connections reflects highly on her ability to manage others. She feels more engaged, focused, and driven in the office as a result of the better personal connections she has, which eventually contributes to an improvement in her leadership qualities and favorably influences her team.

To maintain a good work-life balance, the cultivation of personal connections is not only a luxury but rather a must. You may improve your general health and well-being as well as the quality of your personal relationships if you give your loved ones top priority, actively listen to them, participate in activities they like together, and encourage open communication. Keep in mind that genuine success is not just measured by professional accomplishments but also by the deep ties we establish with the people we value the most. Therefore, commit yourself to mastering the skill of cultivating personal connections and experiencing the happiness and satisfaction that this will bring to both your personal and professional lives.

CONCLUSION

THE IMPORTANCE OF MINDFULNESS IN THE WORKPLACE

The day-to-day grind sometimes includes balancing many occupations at the same time, meeting strict deadlines, and coping with a constant stream of new information. This is true no matter what role you play in the production process: manager, worker, owner, or manufacturer. If this is not effectively regulated, it may soon bring on emotions of anxiety, concern, and burnout. On the other hand, if you incorporate mindfulness into your daily work routine, not only will you be able to establish a greater sense of well-being, but you will also be able to boost your overall performance, which means that you will achieve both of these objectives.

Paying attention to the here and now and concentrating one's attention on that moment without judging or responding in any manner to what one sees or experiences is the act of practicing mindfulness. In order to put it into practice, you need to provide nonreactive attention to your ideas, emotions, and sensations rather than reacting to them. The practice of mindfulness, when brought into the workplace, has the potential to have a transformative effect not just on your capacity to focus but also on your creativity, ability to make choices, and overall experience while working.

If you are a manager, you have the power to make the environment at work more attentive, and you should take advantage of this. If you provide your employees with resources and practices that foster mindfulness, you may be able to aid them in efficiently managing their stress and enhancing their general well-being. You may want to consider offering your staff mindfulness training sessions or meditation workshops in order to educate them on the benefits of practicing mindfulness. Make sure that your employees have access to a designated quiet location where they may go to concentrate their attention, recharge their batteries, and take short breaks. Additionally, the introduction of policies that support work-life balance, such as flexible working hours or the chance to work remotely, may contribute to a culture at the workplace that is more conscious of its employees' overall well-being.

Training in mindfulness has the potential to have a significant and beneficial influence on an individual worker's capacity to handle stress and boost overall job satisfaction. If you go about your job with a mindful attitude, you'll find that you become more present in the moment and immersed in what you're doing. This will lead to higher productivity as well as a decreased likelihood of making errors or failing to notice anything significant. If you practice mindfulness, you will be able to clear your mind of distractions and concentrate intently on the task at hand, which will allow you to do your job more quickly and efficiently. This is due to the fact that mindfulness makes it possible for you to totally submerge yourself in the activity at hand.

Employees aren't the only ones who may benefit from mindfulness training in the workplace; company owners and managers can also reap the rewards of this practice. By developing a culture of mindfulness in the workplace, you may improve employee retention and minimize absenteeism at your organization. When an employee feels supported in their entire well-being and has the skills required to manage the stress that they face, they are more likely to stay interested, motivated, and committed to their profession. Because of this, the company will see an improvement in both its individual outcomes and its overall performance.

Consider the example of a manufacturing company that has just started to include mindfulness practices. By providing its workforce with training in mindfulness and by designating certain quiet areas for employees to utilize during breaks, the company fosters an environment in which workers are able to concentrate and reenergize themselves. As a direct result of this transformation, employees are reporting reduced levels of stress, better levels of work satisfaction, and increased levels of productivity. This not only benefits employees on an individual level, but it also contributes to the overall success of the company by reducing staff turnover and boosting overall productivity.

A changed experience at work may benefit not only the managers and workers of a business but also its owners and manufacturers, and all of these parties may profit from the useful tool that is mindfulness. If you adopt a more mindful approach to your employment, you may be able to enhance your overall health and well-being, reduce the amount of stress you feel, and boost your productivity. Not only does the practice of mindfulness in the workplace have a great impact on the individuals who engage in it, but it also provides a positive contribution to the growth and continued existence of the company as a whole. Therefore, adopt a thinking approach and study the many ways in which it may assist you, not only in your professional life but also in your personal life.

TAKING ACTION TOWARD A MORE MINDFUL APPROACH TO MANAGEMENT

In a world that is always loaded with new demands, strict deadlines, and high-pressure conditions, adopting a management style that is more mindful is analogous to taking a deep, cleansing breath of fresh air. In the quest for a more favorable work-life balance, making the decision to place a higher priority on one's own health and happiness, as well as self-awareness and meaningful interactions with others, is an intentional and conscious choice. Leaders have the ability to change their workplaces into havens of increased productivity, less stress, and general pleasure simply by adopting mindfulness into their approach to management.

Imagine a manager who starts out every day by devoting a few minutes to the practice of mindfulness meditation. They have found a comfortable place to sit in the peaceful calm of the early morning, where they concentrate on their breath and monitor their thoughts without passing judgment. This easy practice of mindfulness sets the tone for the day and enables the manager to acquire a deeper sense of self-awareness and emotional intelligence than they could otherwise. As the day progresses, more difficulties surface, impending deadlines become more pressing, and unforeseen roadblocks crop up. However, equipped with a heightened level of mindfulness, the manager confronts each circumstance with clarity, calm, and the capacity to respond rather than react.

Effective communication is also included in the scope of mindful management, which goes beyond one's own personal practice. The conscientious manager is aware of the need to maintain true connections with both workers and colleagues in order to maintain harmony within the workplace. They take the time to be active listeners, giving others' problems, thoughts, and comments their full and undivided attention while doing so. A culture of respect and cooperation may be fostered in an organization by a manager who practices mindfulness and cultivates an environment that is conducive to open discourse. Employees are given the opportunity to express their opinions, make contributions based on their one-of-a-kind perspectives, and experience true appreciation as vital parts of the team because of the atmosphere that has been created.

In addition, thoughtful manager understands the need to maintain distinct lines of demarcation between their personal lives and their professional lives. They are aware that being constantly connected might result in feelings of exhaustion and a reduction in one's overall productivity. As a result, they encourage the members of their team to make self-care a top priority, putting an emphasis on the value of rest, relaxing, and engaging in activities outside of work that are beneficial to their health. A mindful manager ensures that their staff has the chance to recharge and bring their best selves to the office by advocating for a healthy work-life balance. This allows the employees to bring their best selves to work.

The advantages of using a mindful approach to management are not restricted to a single member of the staff; rather, they accrue to every member of the group as a whole. A company that cultivates mindfulness via activities like meditation and yoga has been shown to have increased productivity, higher morale, and decreased stress levels. When managers make the well-being of their employees a top priority and demonstrate attentive conduct, they set a strong example for the members of their team. When a leader demonstrates enhanced attention, inventiveness, and a sense of purpose in their job, employees are more inclined to follow suit and engage in their work with those same qualities. This good ripple effect spreads across the business, improving cooperation, creativity, and overall pleasure.

Incorporating mindfulness into the world of management is a transformative journey that has significant value for both the managers and the teams that they oversee. Managers are able to build workplaces that encourage personal development, minimize stress, and promote optimum performance when they embrace mindfulness practices such as meditation, effective communication, and a dedication to work-life balance. A manager who practices mindfulness is aware that the success of the company as a whole is directly influenced by the health and happiness of the people under their supervision. Managers have the ability to develop healthy workplaces through the practice of mindfulness. These workplaces will allow people to thrive, teams to thrive, and work to become an activity that is satisfying and sustainable.

For the Manager:

1. **Improved Decision Making:** Mindfulness practices help managers to focus their attention and reduce distractions. This allows them to think more clearly and make better decisions.

2. **Increased Productivity:** Mindfulness practices help managers to reduce stress and improve their ability to prioritize tasks. This can lead to increased productivity and better time management.

3. **Enhanced Communication:** Mindfulness practices can improve communication skills by helping managers to be more present and attentive during conversations. This can lead to better relationships with team members and improved collaboration.

4. **Better Conflict Resolution:** Mindfulness practices can help managers to stay calm and focused during difficult

situations, making it easier to resolve conflicts and find solutions.

For the Team:

1. **Improved Morale:** When managers practice mindfulness, they are more likely to create a positive work environment that promotes well-being and reduces stress. This can lead to improved morale and job satisfaction among team members.

2. **Increased Creativity:** Mindfulness practices can enhance creativity by helping team members to tap into their creative potential and think outside the box.

3. **Better Work-Life Balance:** When managers prioritize mindfulness, they are more likely to encourage their team members to do the same. This can lead to a better work-life balance for everyone on the team.

4. **Improved Performance:** When team members feel supported and valued, they are more likely to perform at their best. Mindful managers can create a culture of trust and respect that promotes high performance.

Mindfulness practices can have a positive impact on both the manager and the team. By prioritizing mindfulness, managers can improve decision-making, productivity, communication, and conflict resolution. In turn, team members can experience improved morale, increased creativity, better work-life balance, and improved performance.

www.ingramcontent.com/pod-product-compliance
Lightning Source LLC
Chambersburg PA
CBHW051256250726

48656CB00004B/1328